VIKING EAST ANGLIA

TIM PESTELL

PREFACE AND ACKNOWLEDGEMENTS

This short book owes its origins to the exhibition *Viking: Rediscover the Legend* on display at Norwich Castle Museum and Art Gallery in 2019. A partnership exhibition between York Museums Trust and The British Museum, and featuring many of the most iconic objects of the period, it shows how our knowledge of those Scandinavian raiders, traders, immigrants and adventurers who came to the British Isles continues to be refined by new discoveries and scientific advances. Equally, this book owes its inspiration to Sue Margeson's *The Vikings in Norfolk*, published in 1997. Sue, a former Keeper of Archaeology at Norwich Castle, was thus a predecessor of mine and the person who, as a Viking scholar, first recognised the quantity of Scandinavian objects being found by metal-detectorists in Norfolk. From them, she argued the finds provided good evidence for Viking immigration and settlement in the region, despite the lack of documentary evidence for this. Not all scholars accepted her case at the time, and indeed one individual even commented of Suffolk that 'sadly, the Danes .. must remain a figment in the imagination of nineteenth-century antiquarians'. The continued recovery and recording of finds has become a tidal wave of data, channelled with the establishment of the Portable Antiquities Scheme. A new generation of scholars has used these new finds in increasingly sophisticated ways to explore the presence and role of the Vikings in English history and it is these stories that the *Viking: Rediscover the Legend* exhibition, and this book, aims to tell.

In offering up this account, I am well aware that there are already many books on the Vikings available (probably too many) and I hesitate to add yet another. However, there has been no updated narrative looking at the region's Viking past since *The Vikings in Norfolk*, and it is increasingly clear that to understand the interaction of these incomers with the native Anglo-Saxon population we need to look at the East Anglian kingdom as a whole, rather than be divided along county lines. That brings with it a swathe of people to whom I am grateful for their kind support and patience over the years while working as an archaeologist and museum curator in the region, by answering questions, providing information and discussing finds and their interpretation.

In particular I am grateful to my colleagues, past and present, working on the front line identifying the eye-wateringly large number of finds made and brought in for identification by the region's metal-detectorists: Steven Ashley, Andrew Brown, Garry Crace, Erica Darch, Helen Geake, Jason Gibbons, Adrian Marsden, Faye Minter, Andrew Rogerson and Julie Shoemark. For their knowledge and discussion of the excavated material I am additionally grateful to Brian Ayers and Keith Wade. While we stand on Sue Margeson's shoulders for Norwich Castle's exceptional collection of Viking material, she would be amazed and delighted to see the number and range of new finds that have emerged in the last twenty years and I would therefore like to give particular thanks to all those metal-detectorists who have allowed their finds to be recorded: in doing so, they have shared rather than wasted the knowledge bound up in them.

Inevitably, staging large exhibitions like *Viking: Rediscover the Legend* are expensive and we therefore kindly acknowledge the financial support of the Dorset Foundation. Likewise for their financial assistance in helping Norwich Castle to acquire many of the outstanding items seen in the following pages we would like to thanks the Friends of Norwich Museums, The V&A/Arts Council Purchase Grant Fund, The Headley Trust, The Art Fund and National Heritage Memorial Fund. As a curator I am particularly grateful to those many metal-detectorists who have followed a rich tradition in generously donating their finds to the county collections.

For their help in bringing this book to publication I owe especial thanks to a number of colleagues, in particular for allowing images of their own museums' Viking objects to be published here: Andrew Woods of York Museums Trust; Eleanor Chant, Joe Edwards, Gareth Williams and especially Beatriz Waters of the British Museum; Jody Joy and Imogen Gunn of the Cambridge Museum of Archaeology and Anthropology; Carolyn Wingfield of Saffron Walden Museum; Glynn Davis, Anna Mercer and Isobel Keith, Colchester and Ipswich Museums Service; Glynis Baxter, West Suffolk Heritage Services; Faye Minter of Suffolk County Council and

Steven Ashley of Norfolk's Finds Identification and Recording Service. For other photos I should like to thank Roland Harris, North Walsham Rugby Club and Hywel Jones.

Most of the items pictured here are in the Norwich Castle collections and I have not individually credited these images, nor material derived from the county's excavation reports or my own photos. From within Norfolk Museums Service I would like to thank colleagues John Davies, Fi Hitchcock and Maria Wong; and Neville Rolt and Steve Hayes of printers Blackmore Group for their help and patience in meeting the exceptionally tight publication timetable. Similarly, I would like to thanks Lesley Abrams, Brian Ayers and Andrew Rogerson for so kindly reading and commenting on the draft text with such speed, although naturally any mistakes appearing here are not their fault but mine. Finally, this book is dedicated to Sara for all her love and support.

Published by Norfolk Museums Service, April 2019
Printed by Blackmore Group, Shaftesbury
ISBN 0903101912

CONTENTS

INTRODUCTION

Most people have heard of the Vikings, and it is hard to escape the image of daring raiders setting out in longships to pillage treasure. They are also known as intrepid explorers, who spread out from Scandinavia and reached across Europe, through Russia to the Islamic world, north to Greenland and Iceland, and even ventured as far west as America. We therefore all have some impression of who or what they were. However, getting beneath this picture to understand their involvement in England requires us to investigate historical and archaeological sources more closely. In particular, new finds and research are rewriting our knowledge of how they interacted with the Anglo-Saxons and had such a powerful role in shaping English history. This short book will look at what happened in East Anglia, one of the wealthiest areas of Anglo-Saxon England and, crucially, one of the places most affected by sea-borne Vikings due to its long coastline (Fig. 1). In doing so we will see how much the Vikings - used in this book in the general sense of people from the Scandinavian world - helped to shape the region, which for much of the Anglo-Saxon period was a kingdom with its own identity and rulers.

To start with though, we need to see where and when the Vikings first appeared. For historians, their arrival is marked by an entry in the *Anglo-Saxon Chronicle* for 793AD:

> In this year terrible portents appeared over Northumbria, and miserably frightened the inhabitants: these were exceptional flashes of lightning, and fiery dragons were seen flying in the air. A great famine soon followed these signs; and a little after that in the same year on 8th June the harrying of the heathen miserably destroyed God's church in Lindisfarne by rapine and slaughter.

The terrible portents of doom are of course as much a literary device used by the writer to emphasise the terror and exceptional nature of these events, a position enabled by hindsight. However as interesting as this notice in the *Chronicle* is that for the next year, which is less frequently mentioned:

> 794. And Northumbria was ravaged by the heathen, and Ecgfrith's monastery at *Donemuþe* [Jarrow] looted: and there one of their leaders was slain, and some of their ships besides were shattered by storms; and many of them were drowned there and some came ashore alive and were at once slain at the river mouth.

This is interesting not only in showing that the raid of 793 was followed up the next year, again on the Northumbrian coast, and again on a monastery, but that the heathen raiders did not have it all their own way. Battle had clearly been joined for one of the leaders to have been killed, while the English equally showed no mercy on those shipwrecked. If the success of 793 had encouraged a number of ships to return the following year, 794's relative failure may have concentrated minds. It was not to stop the raiding however. While it was another forty years before the *Chronicle* again recorded the appearance of 'heathens' (when in 835 they devastated Sheppey), other sources demonstrate there was no let-up. Perhaps just as important is to remember that the intervening time was not a period of tranquillity and calm for England. Instead we need to remember that 'England' did not exist at this time, but was instead a patchwork of separate kingdoms known from early twelfth century as the 'Heptarchy' after its seven most prominent constituents: Wessex, Mercia, Kent, Northumbria, East Anglia, Essex and Sussex. These kingdoms were perpetually in conflict with one another. Wars, raiding and a struggle for military and economic superiority were very much normal features of Anglo-Saxon life, and it was into this mix that the Vikings stepped.

▽ Fig. 1
ANGLO-SAXON ENGLAND AND ITS NORTH SEA NEIGHBOURS IN THE VIKING AGE.

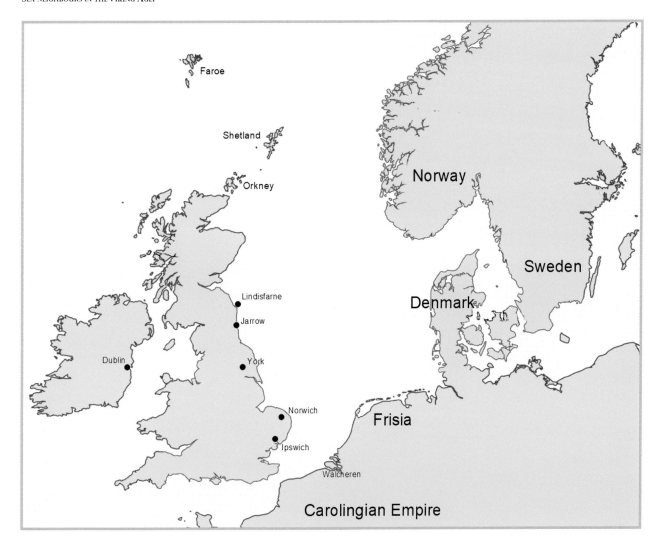

THE KINGDOM OF THE EAST ANGLES

East Anglia has come to mean many different things in the modern world. For the Anglo-Saxons, it had a far more definite meaning, even if placing it accurately on a map is difficult. For many writers at the time the term they used was actually 'the kingdom of the East Angles', in other words a recognition that this was a grouping of peoples as much as a strictly defined block of land (Fig. 2). Exactly who these East Angles were is more difficult to say although perhaps the easiest division is provided by the modern counties of Norfolk and Suffolk, the North and South 'folk' of this kingdom. What is likely is that within this subdivision – probably created in the tenth century – there were smaller tribal units almost certainly ultimately based on the Anglo-Saxon migration period of the fifth and sixth centuries. Names such as the *Happingas* and *Blythingas*, which gave their names to the later Hundreds of Happing in Norfolk (centred upon Happisburgh) and Blything in Suffolk (based upon Blythburgh), point to the relatively small size of such units. Likewise, the *Tribal Hideage*, a document of disputed date but possibly eighth-century origin, names a variety of small tribal groups in the Fenland area. Together, these speak of groups of people ruled or owing services and taxes to leaders that we describe as kings. With the rise and fall of such kings, control might be extended or surrendered, and with it their control over areas of land.

It is, therefore, difficult for us to say exactly where the boundaries of East Anglia lay at the start of Viking activity here. For the Anglo-Saxon monk Bede, writing in the early eighth century, the kingdom extended at least as far as Ely, although the Cambridge area seems to have been a separate political unit. While the coast provided northern and eastern edges, the fens therefore provided a western border area. The southern boundary is likewise uncertain. Modern Essex is clearly named after the kingdom of the East Saxons, but the exact border is unclear and probably lay along the county line of the river Stour: the creation of these county divisions in the Late Anglo-Saxon period presumably rested on earlier meaningful boundaries. This kingdom of the East Angles was to exist as a political unit for much of the Anglo-Saxon period and, as we will see, was to be influenced profoundly by Viking involvement at both political and social levels.

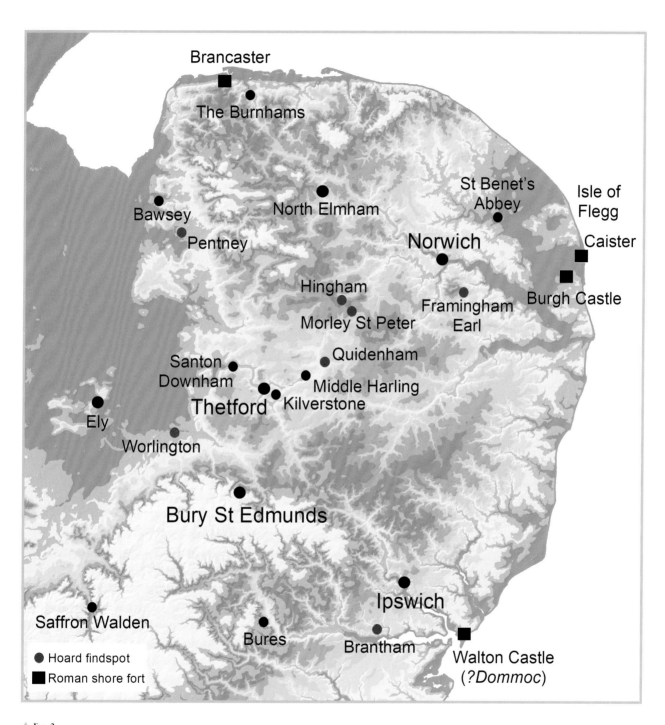

Brancaster

The Burnhams

Bawsey

Pentney

North Elmham

St Benet's
Abbey

Isle of
Flegg

Caister

Norwich

Hingham

Morley St Peter

Framingham
Earl

Burgh Castle

Quidenham

Santon
Downham

Middle Harling

Thetford Kilverstone

Ely

Worlington

Bury St Edmunds

Ipswich

Saffron Walden

Bures

Brantham

Walton Castle
(*?Dommoc*)

● Hoard findspot
■ Roman shore fort

▲ Fɪɢ. 2

Tʜᴇ Kɪɴɢᴅᴏᴍ ᴏꜰ Eᴀsᴛ Aɴɢʟɪᴀ ᴡɪᴛʜ ᴘʟᴀᴄᴇs ᴏꜰ ɪᴍᴘᴏʀᴛᴀɴᴄᴇ ᴍᴇɴᴛɪᴏɴᴇᴅ ɪɴ ᴛʜᴇ ᴛᴇxᴛ.

THE VIKINGS ARRIVE

Anglo-Saxon East Anglia has long been recognised as having a rich archaeology but a poor historical record, with only a few records surviving from the kingdom. The blame for this is often laid at the door of the Vikings, one historian wryly commenting that 'Danes and charters did not get on well together'. While monasteries proved the most obvious keepers for all manner of written documents, they were also the wealthy institutions recorded as being ransacked most frequently. As they were often places where our historical accounts were written, one could hardly blame our documentary sources for being biased by the writers, anxious monks worried about their churches being torn apart. With this in mind, we can use a variety of chronicles and other shorter documents, many of post Norman Conquest date but copying or drawing upon older accounts still then surviving, to reconstruct the increasing Viking presence in East Anglia.

Given East Anglia's long coastline, it is reasonable to assume that the kingdom had been suffering the same sorts of raids detailed elsewhere in the *Anglo-Saxon Chronicle*, with shiploads of 'heathen' conducting quick

▼ FIG. 3

SKELETON 541 UNDERGOING EXCAVATION AT BAWSEY, WEST NORFOLK IN 1998. RADIOCARBON CENTRES ON A DATE OF 760-880 FOR THE BODY WHICH HAD A CHOP-WOUND TO THE SKULL.

raids before withdrawing, only to pop up again elsewhere. To date, no archaeological evidence for such raiding has been found, and given the nature of the hit-and-run tactics employed it is unlikely that it could be recognised as such anyway. For instance, excavations at Bawsey in west Norfolk revealed two interesting skeletons on the site of a high-status settlement, showing evidence of wounds consistent with being attacked with bladed weapons (Fig. 3). Radiocarbon dating showed the young- to middle-aged adult female and male dated to the Middle Anglo-Saxon or early Viking period. However, the broad dating and constant warfare of the age means that it is impossible to attribute their wounds to the Vikings, let alone the same incident.

East Anglia's absence from mention in sources is most probably due to the more localised focus of the *Anglo-Saxon Chronicle's* compilers, which especially show interest in West Saxon affairs. As if to underline it, this is the same period for which the reigning king of the East Angles, Æthelstan,

FIG. 4 ▷

PENNY OF KING ÆTHELSTAN OF EAST ANGLIA. THE SHIP MOTIF, UNIQUE AMONG ANGLO-SAXON COINAGE, IMITATES A SIMILAR DESIGN USED ON CONTEMPORARY CAROLINGIAN ISSUES.

is known only from coins (Fig. 4). Despite this relative invisibility and obscurity, his coinage is reasonably prolific and suggests a king whose reign of about eighteen years (from c.827 - c.845) must have been stable and effective. He may even have been responsible for freeing his kingdom from the overlordship of neighbouring Mercia, following the death of their short-lived King Ludeca (825-7).

The first encounter with the Vikings recorded for East Anglia came in 841 in Æthelstan's reign when

> in this year Ealdorman Herebehrt was killed by heathen men and many men with him in [Romney] Marsh; and later in the same year many men in Lindsey, East Anglia and Kent were killed by the enemy.

By the 850s the situation with the Vikings had worsened still further. In 850-1 the *Chronicle* records that 'For the first time, heathen men stayed through the winter on Thanet'. This tactic of overwintering in England marked a strategic change by the Vikings who were clearly now confident – and presumably strong enough – to stay in England all year. This is an important shift as it not only made them less mobile and easier to pin down for battle, but meant they were less able to live off the land as they moved about. Clearly, some form of provisioning for a force substantial enough to protect itself was possible, again suggesting some links to local communities to extract renders of food and fodder. 865 saw the arrival in the autumn of 'a great heathen army'. In East Anglia, the reigning king was now a man called Eadmund (or Edmund), who had succeeded Æthelweard as king c.855.

The story of Eadmund is fascinating and has been the source of much mythologizing, as the king quickly came to be considered a saint. In death he attained far more significance and power than he had ever had in life, because of how he could be portrayed by others (Fig. 5). This means it has been exceptionally hard to determine what about his life and actions is fact or fiction. Even Eadmund's date of succession, Christmas Day 855, is not certain. It is provided by *The Annals of St Neots*, a document written *c.*1120-40, at Bury St Edmunds abbey. Because these annals contain other important pieces of information and traditions that may have been preserved by the community at Bury – unsurprising given their particular interest in Eadmund – this date of 855 has been generally accepted. The annal for 855 also contains the detail that Eadmund was consecrated as king by Bishop Hunberht at a royal estate called *Burna*. Subsequent historical accounts had changed the name to *Burum* by the middle of the twelfth century when Geoffrey of Wells began to write about St Edmund. From this, *Burum* was associated with Bures St Mary on the Suffolk-Essex border, and this was the actual place-name used by Matthew Paris by 1230. However, not only does Domesday Book of 1086 give the spelling of Bures as *Bura*, there is little evidence to support this place as once having been a royal estate where such a coronation might be expected to have taken place. By contrast, a location in north Norfolk suggests itself far more strongly as the possible location for Eadmund being crowned. Burnham is now a collection of seven individual parishes which were clearly once a larger land unit, and where archaeological evidence suggests there had been an early and rich estate – exactly the sort of place a king might base himself. Moreover, our earliest place-names from here (again from Domesday Book) have forms closer to our *Burna*: *Bruneham*, *Brunaham* and, from 1121, *Burneham*. Perhaps significantly, the Burnhams came to have churches dedicated to St Edmund and another East Anglian saintly king, Æthelberht, exactly what one might expect if this was a royal centre memorialising former members of the family line.

The place-name evidence is not clear but an interesting additional feature is that Eadmund's crowning was undertaken by Bishop Hunberht. When he was made king, there were two bishoprics in East Anglia, once based in the south of the kingdom at *Dommoc*, probably at Walton Castle in Suffolk, and one in the north at Elmham, now North Elmham in Norfolk. We have no evidence that there was ever any 'superior' see between the two bishops in the kingdom, although if there were, one might suppose it would have been the bishop of *Dommoc* as this was older established. Yet, Eadmund was made

Sc̄ Edmund

king by Hunberht of Elmham rather than the southern bishop, at the time probably Æthelwold. There are historical problems as these two men are the last recorded bishops of *Dommoc* and Elmham before a gap caused by the Viking incursions, and the date when they ceased to be bishops is unknown. However, Hunberht's role in Eadmund's coronation provides another clue that should lead us to look for *Burna* being in Norfolk not Suffolk, and strengthens Burnham's claim as the site.

If this all seems hedged in by ifs and buts, it really reflects just how poor and difficult our historical sources are for East Anglia at this date. The next stepping-stone we have to reconstruct Eadmund's time as king is more certain. In its typically brief way, the *Anglo-Saxon Chronicle* records how in 865

> And the same year a great heathen army came into England and took up winter quarters in East Anglia; and there they were supplied with horses, and the East Angles made peace with them.

Eadmund would seem to have done much the same as many other Anglo-Saxon kings did in the face of the Vikings — he bought them off to go into a rival kingdom elsewhere. The buying of peace, which was to become such a familiar theme with Vikings, could have mixed results. When the people of Kent tried to do this the previous year, the historian Asser records that:

> under cover of that peace and promise of money, the [Viking] army stole away inland by night and ravaged all eastern Kent for they knew that they would seize more money by secret plunder than by peace

In Eadmund's case, the Vikings did go, moving out as a mobile war-band to Northumbria the following year, to the city of York.

A possible witness to this period of uncertainty in the kingdom is a coin-hoard of silver pennies of Eadmund found by a metal-detectorist in the parish of Worlington, near Thetford, in Suffolk (Fig. 6). Sadly, only a fraction of the hoard was declared to the authorities, but one responsible metal-detectorist working there has now found nine coins, struck by five moneyers: Æthelwulf, Beonferth, Eadmund, Sigeræd and Twicga. These moneyers all seem to have worked in the earlier period of Eadmund's reign and the fact that the hoard consists only of his coins suggests that it was an assemblage collected locally, and put into the ground by an East Anglian rather than a passing Viking. That the owner never returned for

KING EADMUND AS REPRESENTED ON THE LATE FIFTEENTH-CENTURY ROOD SCREEN IN LUDHAM CHURCH, NORFOLK.

their money perhaps speaks of the violence accompanying the Viking army's overwintering.

According to tradition, the leaders fighting Eadmund were Ivar and Hubba, of which Ivar was said to be the son of famous Viking warrior Ragnar Lothbrok. This association of Ivar (also variously called Inwaer or Hinguar) is given by another Anglo-Saxon chronicler, Æthelweard, writing some time between about 978 and 988, and if nothing else reflects the legendary nature of the Vikings involved in this 'Great Army'.

Quite how much freedom Eadmund had as king following the Vikings' departure is unclear. It is probably this last phase of his rule that sees four new moneyers striking coins in his name, namely Beaghelm, Beornheah, Eadberht and Eadwald, and while some earlier individuals like Beornferth, Eadmund and Twicga continued to act as moneyers for a short while, only Sigeræd, a late-comer to Eadmund's earlier coinage, was to last. Coinage

▼ Fig. 6

The Worlington Hoard of Eadmund pennies.

provides one barometer of a kingdom's stability and especially regal control of a significant resource, as among other things, it was a means of exercising taxation and with that control over a population. Eadmund's later coinage saw a decrease in size, a large drop in the silver content having already taken place earlier in his reign. These elements all hint that Eadmund's rule was exercised in difficult circumstances in which his own power may have been circumscribed by the demands of the Viking armies. Indeed, it may be that the Vikings' return to East Anglia was precipitated by Eadmund attempting to assert his independence while the Great Army was preoccupied elsewhere.

This had certainly happened before: in Northumbria, York was captured on November 1st 866 but when the Northumbrians attempted to retake the city in March the following year the Vikings returned, harrying the kingdom as far north as the river Tyne. They established a client king, Egbert, and possibly allowed the Archbishop of York, Wulfhere, to co-operate in rule, as both were subsequently expelled by another native Northumbrian force in 872. Again, the Viking Great Army returned, installing a new king, Ricsige, and restoring Wulfhere. Whatever the reason for the Vikings' return to East Anglia, the consequences for Eadmund were to be severe.

In 869 the Great Army returned, possibly even using the horses the East Anglians had bought them off with. The *Anglo-Saxon Chronicle* recounts:

> In this year the raiding army rode across Mercia into East Anglia, and took up winter quarters at Thetford. And that winter King Eadmund fought against them, and the Danes had the victory, and killed the king and conquered the land.

On the face of it, this account could suggest that Eadmund had died in battle against the Vikings, although this contradicts the later stories written about Edmund as a saint. It is picking a path through the small details in these later accounts that has given historians a challenge for many years. These stories were written with the intention of underlining Edmund's saintly status rather than with any concern for historical accuracy in mind. Indeed, the earliest of these accounts was written 116 years after Edmund's death. Called the *Passio Sancti Eadmundi*, the 'Passion of Saint Edmund', it was written by a monk from Fleury in France called Abbo, while he was staying in the fenland abbey of Ramsey between 985-7.

Abbo's narrative tells us how Eadmund was martyred by the Vikings, being tied to a tree and used for archery target practice by the Vikings until his body was so full of arrows that he looked like a 'prickly hedgehog'. They then cut off his head and threw it into a bramble thicket of woods at a place called *Hægelisdun*. When the locals came to retrieve the body, they searched unsuccessfully for Eadmund's head until miraculously it called out 'Here! Here!' They found their king's head being guarded between the paws of a 'guardian wolf'. Placing head and body together again, it rejoined leaving no trace of a scar. According to another author, Archdeacon Hermann (who was writing even later, *c.*1095-1100), Eadmund was buried 'in a little village called Sutton, close to the scene of his martyrdom'. Later, Eadmund's body was then dug up and moved as saintly relics to a place called *Beodricesworth*, today known as Bury St Edmunds, some time during or before the reign of West Saxon King Æthelstan (924-39).

There has been much argument over the years about where Eadmund's martyrdom occurred. While there are a number of villages in Norfolk and Suffolk called Sutton, the place-name *Hægelisdun* is most easily associated

▼ Fig. 7

(Left) Coinage distributions of East Anglian kings Æthelstan and (Right) Eadmund, drawn on data from the online *Corpus of Early Medieval Coin Finds.*

with Hellesdon, near Norwich. The weakness of this is its obvious distance from Bury St Edmunds. An interesting alternative suggestion was put forward by Stanley West in 1984, observing that a field-name of Hellesdon occurred on an 1840 tithe map for the Suffolk parish of Bradfield St Clare, itself two-thirds of a mile (one kilometre) from the place Sutton Hall – which is only five and a half miles (nine kilometres) from Bury St Edmunds. Not everyone agrees with this identification but it provides a more convincing explanation for why Bury was chosen to take Eadmund's relics. It is also more likely from a wider perspective. When the Vikings overwintered in East Anglia in 869 they chose to locate themselves in Thetford, a town that was strategically important within the kingdom, as well as being astride a navigable river, the Ouse, which provided excellent communications. It seems possible that Thetford had become politically important by this time. While we do not know where East Anglia's coinage was being struck at this date, numismatists (on few particularly good grounds) suggest Ipswich, yet the distribution of coins issued by Eadmund and indeed his predecessors Æthelweard and Æthelstan, focus not on south-east Suffolk and Ipswich but upon central East Anglia – and Thetford (Fig. 7). By contrast, the coinage of Eadwald (c.796-8) suggests a distribution with slight concentrations in south-east Suffolk and north-west Norfolk, a pattern more familiar from earlier eighth-century coinage when Ipswich was the major trading town of the kingdom. It is perhaps significant that Worlington, site of the Eadmund penny hoard, is only 12½ miles from Thetford and a second hoard of Eadmund's coins, along with jewellery, has been found at Hingham in Norfolk, some 7 miles from Thetford (see box description). With Bury St Edmunds only 11 miles from Thetford and 5 miles from Sutton, these suggest the power centre of the kingdom over which Eadmund and the Vikings were contesting.

The Hingham Hoard is a remarkable collection of four silver brooches, two silver strap-ends and twenty-three pennies of Eadmund of East Anglia. (Fig A) Although much damaged by being in ploughsoil before being recovered by metal-detectorists, they illustrate the wealth someone was desperate to conceal in the closing years of Eadmund's reign.

The brooches include a now fragmentary openwork silver disc brooch in the form of an equal-armed cross with splayed terminals to the arms (Fig. B). About a quarter survives, including the central roundel, a fragment of surviving cross-arm, and a joining fragment with a complete cross-arm and parts of two openwork panels between the arms. The cross is divided into a number of decorative panels, each containing ninth-century 'Trewhiddle'-style decoration with a background of niello. The narrow bands of silver separating the fields are often decorated with a line of punched circular dots, or 'speckling', with engraved guide lines visible in one place. Enough survives of the brooch to show that it was originally a spectacular piece, some 68mm in diameter yet with a thickness of less than 1mm.

▲ Fig. B
DISC BROOCH FRAGMENT.

FIG. C ▷

DISC BROOCH FROM THE PENTNEY HOARD.
© THE TRUSTEES OF THE BRITISH MUSEUM.

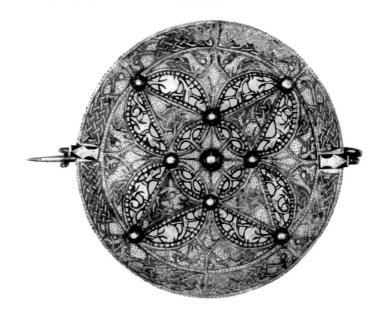

▲ FIG. D
'BAG-BELLIED BEAST' DETAIL FROM THE
PENTNEY BROOCH.
© THE TRUSTEES OF THE BRITISH MUSEUM.

▲ FIG. E
COPPER-ALLOY TRIAL-PIECE FROM BAWSEY.

One of the closest parallels to this brooch is a similar silver disc brooch also found in Norfolk, in Pentney in 1977 (Fig. C). This gives some idea of how magnificent the Hingham brooch must once have been and that it was of the very best craftsmanship. It also shares a feature of 'bag-bellied' Trewhiddle animals (Fig. D) which may suggest that it was made in East Anglia, as a craft-worker's trial-piece showing a similar animal also comes from Norfolk, from Bawsey (Fig. E).

A second brooch from the hoard is also unusual, being an openwork design made from very thin sheet silver. The centre has an undecorated square panel with a separate dome-headed silver rivet around which are four square apertures, and from the central square extend flanged lines, both running along the four cardinal lines, with flanking tear-like extensions. The overall design probably represented a cross-shape, as can be seen in the suggested reconstruction (Fig. F). The construction of very thin sheet silver is curious and the reverse has deposits that might be traces of solder, suggesting that the silver openwork is actually the front of a brooch with a separate, perhaps copper-alloy, back-plate.

Another of the Hingham brooches, more corroded, is likewise similar to other East Anglian Trewhiddle-style products, notably two silver brooches from Chediston and Elmsett in Suffolk (Fig. G).

The two silver strap-ends are unusual finds. Strap-ends are metal fittings that were used at the end of straps of various types in the Anglo-Saxon period, probably ranging from belts and garters to attachment straps on sword scabbards and bags.

▲ Fig. F

RECONSTRUCTION OF THE OPENWORK SILVER BROOCH
FROM HINGHAM. *BY ERICA DARCH.*

▲ Fig. G

RECONSTRUCTION OF THE ELMSETT BROOCH.
© *SUFFOLK COUNTY COUNCIL.*

The two examples here are so similar in style, especially with their serrated-edges, that they were quite probably made in the same workshop (Fig. H). Silver strap-ends are not only rare, but are high-status dress accessories. Here, they have animals outlined in niello in their main panels, but they are marked out by their animal-head ends having inlaid blue-glass eyes – a small detail that would have brought the beasts alive by sparkling in the light and appealing to the Anglo-Saxons' love of tiny, delicate, details.

Interestingly, the Hingham Hoard seems to be English not Viking. The jewellery is all Anglo-Saxon and the large brooch seems to use Eastern English, if not local, variants of the Trewhiddle style. The coins likewise are all East Anglian and the fact that ten different moneyers are represented in the twenty-three pennies suggests that this was a hoard gathered from everyday circulation rather than freshly-minted coin where we could expect batches of identical examples. That all the coins were those of Eadmund may also suggest that the coinage then circulating in the kingdom was relatively well-controlled and therefore not featuring 'foreign' English coins from other kingdoms.

Much like the spectacular Pentney Hoard of brooches, it is impossible to know the precise reasons for the Hingham Hoard's deposition. While we cannot rule out some other less specific (and perhaps more personal) circumstance, the composition and date of the hoard makes it most likely to relate to the Vikings' reappearance in East Anglia in 869. This strongly suggests that the Hingham Hoard was put into the ground by a local, English, person to safeguard it against Viking looting. That it was never recovered is perhaps a reminder of the very real dangers presented by the Vikings' presence.

▲ Fig. H

THE TWO STRAP-ENDS.

FIG. 8

A PENNY OF THE OTHERWISE UNKNOWN KING
ÆTHELRED OF EAST ANGLIA, STRUCK BY THE
MONEYER EADWALD, FROM BRACON ASH,
NORFOLK.

In the short term Eadmund's death presented the Viking army with the issue of how to maintain their control over the East Anglian populace. Their response seems to have followed previous practice, by establishing a 'client' king. The silence of historical sources means that our knowledge of this period is drawn only from coinage; seven coins are known which were issued by a man named Æthelred (Fig. 8), and another two by someone called Oswald (Fig. 9). Which of these men came first is unknown, or indeed whether East Anglia was somehow divided between the two. Most likely Æthelred was the successor to Eadmund and of these coins we have the name of four moneyers (Beornheah, Eadwald, Heahmod and Sigered), who had also struck coins for Eadmund. We know nothing about who Æthelred or Oswald were, but these coins suggest that while the issues of Æthelred are exceptionally rare, they may suggest a reasonable output of coinage under him, and thus some continuity in royal functions from Eadmund. In effect, they help further the historical interpretation that Æthelred was a 'real' king in the region.

While later stories of St Eadmund describe him as a virgin martyr, this may have been no more than a detail to emphasise his saintliness – it was also convenient to the West Saxon kings who came to rule England, to stop claims from any East Anglian aristocratic family for the East Anglian throne. Indeed, it is possible that Æthelred was from a rival dynastic family to Eadmund. There is some evidence that families chose names with similar forms and so there may have been a family relationship between Æthelred and the Æthelweard whom Eadmund succeeded. This much is speculation. More certain is what happened next to the kingdom.

FIG. 9 ▷

PENNY OF OSWALD OF EAST
ANGLIA, DISCOVERED WITHIN
THE CUERDALE HOARD.
© THE TRUSTEES OF THE
BRITISH MUSEUM.

In 878 the Viking Great Army was finally stopped by King Alfred 'The Great' of Wessex, at the Battle of Edington. The peace that was subsequently sealed, the Treaty of Wedmore, saw an agreement over areas of political interest. A sign of Alfred's victory was the obligation for the Viking leader, Guthrum, to be baptised. At the time it was no more certain that this peace would be held than any of the previous agreements made by Anglo-Saxon kings with the Vikings: only subsequent events allowed the Anglo-Saxon writers to present their accounts with the benefit of hindsight, making it appear this way. The Vikings under Guthrum moved on from Chippenham to Cirencester in the west, while another Viking warband arrived in England, encamping next to the Thames at Fulham. Two years later, in 880, the Vikings returned to East Anglia and, crucially, they 'shared out the land'. Notably, the Fulham-based Vikings were not part of this, instead sailing abroad to Ghent to try their luck in the Frankish kingdom.

This arguably marks a turning-point in the Viking experience in England, as they now ended their constant movement from kingdom to kingdom. What it did not do was see an end to conflict between the Vikings and, in particular, the West Saxon kingdom. Sources make it clear that 'war bands' operated out of the eastern areas under Danish control, known later as the Danelaw, and raids were at times launched from here in support of Viking campaigns elsewhere. In 885 Alfred had sent a naval force to East Anglia where it defeated a force of 16 ships before then encountering, and losing to, another Viking force. Their pursuit into East Anglia had, according to the chronicler Æthelweard, been occasioned by the Vikings twice breaking promises after coming to terms with Alfred, and because the force had been aided by Danes settled in East Anglia. Again, in 894 a Danish force retreated from Wales, via Northumbria, to East Anglia so that English forces 'were unable to get at them'.

The most potent symbol of the Vikings' settlement in East Anglia is arguably the removal of their client king and replacement by Guthrum himself, now striking coins in his English baptismal name of Æthelstan (Fig. 10). The choice of this name could be significant as it is not one that has an obviously exclusive relationship with Alfred or his West Saxon family. However, in an East Anglian context it directly recalls the Æthelstan who, as we have seen, may have reasserted East Anglian independence from Mercia and whose long reign presumably reflects his political and military abilities. As all parents know, the choice of a name for a child is not a random process and such a loaded symbolic act as baptism would have meant that any new name would have been very carefully selected and charged with significance. Guthrum may therefore have deliberately chosen this name to attach to himself some notion of East Anglian identity in recognition of his claim to rule the kingdom.

While East Anglia remained a place under Danish influence, elsewhere the West Saxon kings were slowly reasserting English control, perhaps aided by the fact the Vikings were no longer a mobile force but were settled in territories. The point at which East Anglia also succumbed to this advance still cannot be seen clearly. In 917 the *Anglo-Saxon Chronicle* records that

> King Edward went with the West Saxon levies to Colchester … many people, both from East Anglia and from Essex, who had previously been under Danish domination submitted to him, and the entire Danish army in East Anglia swore union with him.

A political accommodation is clearly indicated, but in the best political speak, swearing 'union' is not the same as 'submitting' to Edward. While many East Anglians perhaps wanted to submit to another Englishman, this is by no means certain. Likewise, the identification of the Danish army being a coherent group and swearing union shows the political control of the area was still contested. Another illustration of this is demonstrated by the rise of the cult of St Edmund.

FIG. 10 ▶
PENNY OF GUTHRUM/
ÆTHELSTAN OF EAST ANGLIA.
© *THE TRUSTEES OF THE
BRITISH MUSEUM.*

THE RISE OF ST EDMUND

If creating a client king had given the Vikings an immediate solution to Eadmund's removal, it was to have far greater long-term implication. Written accounts of Eadmund's saintly life and associated miracles first appear in the later tenth century, but a more direct testament to the rise of his cult is the appearance of a 'memorial' coinage. They provide unequivocal evidence for the promotion of a cult celebrating Eadmund as a saint. Starting in about 895, the design of the Edmund memorial pennies copied the coinage of Eadmund himself, but with the legend SCE EADMVND REX – 'O St Edmund the King!' (Fig. 11). The coinage was prolific, with over 2,000 examples known, produced by over 70 different moneyers, and with a distribution concentrated across East Anglia and the Midlands. Several places were probably involved as mints before Edward the Elder's conquest of the Midlands in 917/18, when East Anglian moneyers came to strike coins in Edward's name.

For such a coinage to have appeared in the first place, Eadmund's cult must have become both popular and important enough to have gained political

◀ FIG. 11

A ST EDMUND MEMORIAL PENNY DISPLAYING A TYPICALLY GARBLED INSCRIPTION. BENEATH THE CENTRAL 'A' CAN BE SEEN A 'PECK-MARK' USED TO DETERMINE THE COIN'S SILVER PURITY.

traction. Less certain is how this was achieved in the 25 years between Eadmund's death and the appearance of the coinage. For the Viking rulers to have adopted St Edmund's name onto their coinage - a king whose death they were responsible for - and to proclaim his saintly status, demonstrates the power of his cult. Equally important, it shows the adoption of an explicitly Christian outlook. Exactly what occasioned this and why is more difficult and inevitably speculative. Most probably it relates to political dissension within East Anglia.

The most obvious context for this presents itself in the death of Guthrum in 890. In a period when kingship and rule depended on military strength and might, the death of a ruler inevitably saw a jockeying for power. For a man as powerful and influential as Guthrum had been, the situation may have been particularly acute. Guthrum's death is dated to 890 by the *Annals of St Neots*, but this was wrongly placed in these annals, if its own statement that he died fourteen – not twelve – years after his baptism in 878 is correct. Potentially, his death was therefore actually in 892, the date one numismatist suggests (on other grounds) was the start-date for the St Edmund memorial coinage. Regardless, the coinage dates to soon after Guthrum's death.

If we accept that the years after Guthrum died were ones of some political tension, and there is no coinage to suggest a clear leader in the old kingdom emerging, then possibly an English East Anglian faction was gaining strength and using the cult of St Edmund as a political banner around which to gather. Whether such a grouping did gain power, or Guthrum's Scandinavian successors, we cannot know, but the striking of coins proclaiming Eadmund a saint was most probably some act of reconciliation. It also marks the end of an East Anglian coinage in which rulership was proclaimed over this kingdom. It was not the end of Viking activity in East Anglia though, nor of the region continuing to have its own social and cultural identity. Crucially, Guthrum's old kingdom was now occupied not only by Anglo-Saxon peoples but Scandinavian settlers. Understanding just how many Vikings came to settle, and therefore the extent of their influence, has been far more problematic for archaeologists and historians. A number of approaches have been made to try and answer this, all with their own difficulties.

PLACE NAMES AND VIKING SETTLEMENT

It has been obvious for a long time that some place-names in East Anglia derive from the Scandinavian language. The argument has therefore been that it was Scandinavian people that were giving these names to places as a result of their settlement. The problem with this form of evidence is that accurately dating exactly *when* such places took on these names is exceptionally difficult. We have already seen how short of documentary history East Anglia is in this period, and for the most part, the earliest evidence we have for the form that place-names took is the Domesday Book, written in 1086 – more than two hundred years after the *Anglo-Saxon Chronicle* tells us the Viking Great Army settled down.

This presents us with a number of problems. First, can we be sure that any Scandinavian place-names belong to this earliest period of Viking settlement rather than, say, a second round of Viking influence under King Cnut in the 1020s? Or, was there so much continued contact with the Scandinavian world that such influences continued into even the twelfth century and therefore obscure the earliest period of settlement? Finally, if we cannot date the forms of name used very accurately, can we actually say anything useful about how many Vikings came over, or later called for their families to join them in East Anglia? Can the form of a name show which language was being used and hence where the settlers were coming from – such as Norwegian or Danish Vikings?

Even with all these problems, there are interesting observations that can be made. Perhaps in the first place, there is clearly a very definite concentration of Scandinavian place-names along the eastern coast and in those inland areas of England that were to become known as the Danelaw. For the great Anglo-Saxon historian Sir Frank Stenton, these names 'are the most obviously significant of all the materials for its history'. Even with all the issues of exactly when and how the names were coined, they demonstrate the huge influence of the Vikings in England, which led to the renaming of places within the landscape.

Scandinavian place-names tend to be made up of two types, topographical and habitative, that is, names describing landscape features and names referring to settlements (Fig. 12). Of the habitative place-names the *–thorp* names are perhaps least indicative of the first stage of Scandinavian settlement, as they developed later in the process of agricultural specialisation and refer to settlements dependent on estate centres. Interestingly, *-thorpe* is not found in those areas where the Vikings were largely of Norwegian extraction, such as north-west England, and the Northern and Western Isles of Scotland. Where it does occur in East Anglia, it would therefore seem to be from Danish influence. Unfortunately, Thorpe can also derive from an English equivalent, as the corresponding word in Old English was –*throp*, and it is not always possible to tell whether the name had an English or Scandinavian origin. It is also the case that new place-names called Thorpe continued to be established even after the Norman Conquest, for instance Thorpe Green in Weasenham St Peter, Norfolk; Thorpe also came to be used in relation to the name of a nearby major village, such as Gayton Thorpe or Burnham Thorpe

So-called 'Grimston-hybrid' names provide a more tantalising Viking origin. Here, a Scandinavian personal name (in the case of Grimston, *Grímr*) was

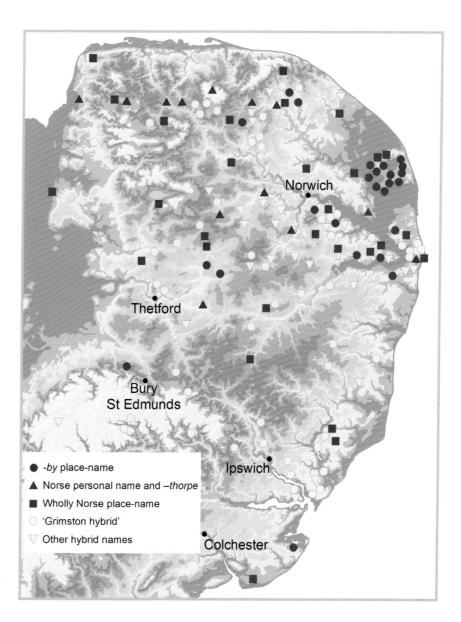

Legend:
● -*by* place-name
▲ Norse personal name and –*thorpe*
■ Wholly Norse place-name
○ 'Grimston hybrid'
▽ Other hybrid names

Norwich

Thetford

Bury
St Edmunds

Ipswich

Colchester

combined with the English word *tūn*, or 'farmstead, village'. While English and Scandinavian personal names did not overlap a great deal in this period, fashion led many English families to adopt Scandinavian names in the eleventh century, just as they were later to do in the wake of the Norman Conquest with names like Stephen and John being preferred to English names like Æthelstan or Wulfric. It is also the case that some Grimston hybrids are formed using vocabulary relating to the landscape, such as tree- or plant-names. Others are again of later date – including some Continental names which were themselves based ultimately on Scandinavian names. With later Viking raiding and ultimately conquest under Danish King Cnut, his followers in the eleventh century may have given their names to some of the existing English *-tun* places.

Despite these problems, it is clear that there is a far higher density of Grimston-hybrid names in Eastern England, suggesting there were more people with Scandinavian names here to be adopted into place-names. There are fewer in East Anglia than further to the north – about 30 each in Norfolk and Suffolk – but their distribution throughout the kingdom suggests that they were used or adopted consistently across the region. What this cannot tell us is when this happened and it is equally notable that these hybrid names are often associated with settlement naming stretching into the post-Conquest period. As evidence for a mass-migration or mass-settlement by recently retired Vikings in the ninth

◀ Fig. 13
Never far from a Viking name in Flegg.

century, the evidence is exceptionally weak, but as evidence of the continuing strength of Scandinavian cultural identity, it is very striking

This leaves us with those names incorporating the –*by* ending, of which there are over 20 in Norfolk, more than half of them in the Isle of Flegg. *Bý* is a standard Old Norse word for 'settlement', which could mean anything from a farm to a village. Where it is found it should perhaps suggest a Scandinavian settlement, especially when it is combined with a Scandinavian personal name, such as in Rollesby (from *Hròðulfr* or *Hrōlfr* - Rolf), Ormesby (from Ormr) or Oby (from the Old Danish personal name *Øthi*), all on the Isle of Flegg. Some *by*-names contain fossilised grammatical endings, indicating that they were formed by people speaking the Norse language. Almost inevitably, there is a 'however'. The place-names we have were recorded in English not Scandinavian sources and so even if some places were known by Scandinavian names to Viking settlers, only those which had passed into wider usage (by the English too) would come to be recorded in Anglo-Saxon or Norman documents. However, although the origin of any single place-name might be questioned, large-scale use of the Norse language particular place-name types tends to argue against this. For the –*by* names of East Anglia, and in particular the Isle of Flegg in Norfolk (Fig. 13), this insistently suggests that such place-names were coined in a predominantly Norse-speaking society.

Could this be evidence for an otherwise undocumented large-scale migration and settlement of Scandinavians? If so, exactly when was this happening, and how and why were such lands going out of English possession? While the evidence is uncertain, study of similar –*by* names in the Midlands and Yorkshire suggests that these names were coined while the Scandinavian language was still being widely spoken, more probably in the ninth and tenth than the eleventh century. Scandinavian linguistic influence also affected existing Old English words: the Old English *mæþl-æsc*, Matlask in Norfolk, (the ash tree where the moot (or meeting) was held), acquiring a hard Scandinavian 'k'. Added to this, the prolific evidence of field-names in such areas suggests that there was a wider Norse-speaking population with a large variety of personal names, giving their names and terminology to the land and natural world they were working within. Thus we find words like *lundr*, a grove, as in Rockland in Norfolk (*Rokelund* in Domesday Book), *eik*, the oak tree, from the Old Danish giving the place-name Eyke in Suffolk, a woodland clearing or meadow like *þveit* giving the name Thwaite in both Norfolk and Suffolk, or *haugr*, a hill or barrow, as in Howe (Norfolk). Likewise a beck or stream, such as the Goose Beck in Burnham, Norfolk, derives from the Old Norse *bekkr*, while the word *-gata* or street became a part of an urban settler's landscape, leading to the modern –gate, seen in many streets in both Norwich and Ipswich (Fig. 14). Eight hundred-names (centres of administration) in Norfolk and two in Suffolk have been identified as Scandinavian in origin, including three around Thetford formed with *haugr* (South Greenhoe, Grimshoe, and Forehoe).

This variety suggests that such names for places arose from a wider immigrant population, rather than a limited elite, imposing their names on the landscape. In this light it is interesting to discuss the remarkable concentration of –*by* names on the Isle of Flegg in east Norfolk. The location of thirteen such names so close together, as well as several other wholly Norse names, is an obviously unusual cluster within the kingdom of East Anglia and suggests that it is the result of some specific event or process, rather than simply being by chance. One possibility is that the area, probably once a low-lying near-island surrounded by marshy fen in the Anglo-Saxon period, was subjected to a mass settlement by Vikings that was otherwise unrecorded. This possibility is an interesting one and certainly deserves serious consideration. A context for such an event is that the kings of East Anglia adopted the policy of Frankish rulers like Lothar, who in 841 ceded the island of Walcheren in Frisia to the Viking leader Harald 'to secure the services' of his army. That is, Lothar bought off the Vikings who had been raiding that stretch of coast by giving them land upon which to settle. In return, it was

◀ FIG. 14

FISHERGATE IN NORWICH, THE STREET OF THE FISHERMEN, WHICH RUNS PARALLEL TO THE RIVER WENSUM.

then their responsibility to defend this same coast against other Viking raiders, which they now had a vested interest in protecting.

There is no historical evidence for such an event at Flegg, but in a region with such poor documentary sources this is no surprise. East Anglia was in close contact with this part of the Continent in the eighth and ninth centuries and may therefore have been receptive to the ideas rulers like Lothar were trying, to stem the same Viking coastal raids. It would also help to explain why there was such an intense and tight cluster of Scandinavian place-names. If it was an early settlement, it might have been more likely to have maintained itself as an enclave of Norse-speakers into the tenth century as the Viking conflict continued, surviving to be adopted into English records. In strictly strategic terms, Flegg may have had a significance, standing to the north of the Great Estuary, which although by now partially silted up gave access to the rivers Yare and Wensum, and had in the Roman period required military 'Saxon Shore' fortifications at Caister and Burgh Castle to defend its entrance from earlier raiding.

There are objections to this idea of course, perhaps the most notable being that we have no evidence in English sources for similar land-grants being made elsewhere in the country to buy off the Vikings. Equally significant, Walcheren was home to the significant trading centre of Domburg, a site that made the island a greater prize to Harald despite the defensive duties it imposed. There is no such evidence on Flegg for an important trading site. Perhaps equally problematic, while there is evidence on Flegg for settlement in both Roman and Anglo-Saxon periods, there is relatively little of the sorts of Viking metalwork that, all things being equal, one might expect in an area that was an enclave of Viking settlers. Given the number of finds now emerging through metal-detecting, this is perhaps surprising. Finally, we need to remember that there may have been other reasons behind Flegg's density of Norse place-names, including perhaps a localised change to the landholding later on, perhaps in the tenth or eleventh centuries. Nevertheless, the clear impression is that this was one part of East Anglia to which a Norse-speaking population had been particularly drawn and maintained a physical presence in their settlements.

IN SEARCH OF THE VIKING DEAD

If some place-names suggest a sufficient number of the population speaking Old Norse to coin new names for settlements, archaeologists have not unreasonably sought evidence for the material remains of these Vikings. In particular, the fact that these people were not Christian meant that in their native Scandinavia, the dead were buried with grave-goods, or objects, that they would have worn or used in life, to accompany them into the afterlife. Christian Anglo-Saxons by contrast, were buried with nothing at this date. Vikings who died in England might be expected to have been treated in the same way as at home, and we should therefore be able to recognise them from their graves in reasonable numbers. For many years the opposite seemed to be the case – that there was actually very little evidence for them. Partly on the basis of this, some people argued that the Vikings had actually come over in far smaller numbers than the Anglo-Saxon sources suggest, and that their presence may have been more of a political one with an elite take-over, rather than large numbers of foot-soldiers and families creating a mass migration of people. Evidence to the contrary is provided by at least one entry in the *Anglo-Saxon Chronicle* when, in 893, King Alfred's forces stormed a viking fort at Benfleet 'and seized everything inside it, both property and women and also children'.

There certainly are examples of Viking cemeteries now beginning to emerge, most notably graves found associated with a camp laid out by the Vikings

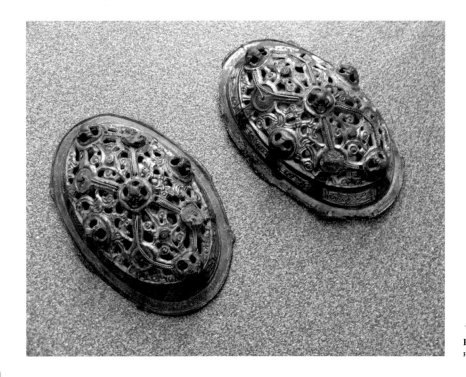

◀ Fig. 15

Pair of oval brooches from a Viking burial found in Santon, Norfolk in 1867.

around the parish church at Repton in Derbyshire where their Great Army overwintered in 873-4. Most conspicuous was a warrior buried with sword and pagan amulets such as a 'Thor's hammer'. Another small cemetery was found at nearby Ingleby Wood, where about 60 Viking mound-burials contained cremations, while in 2004 a small cemetery was found by metal-detectorists at Cumwhitton in Cumbria. Finding similar Scandinavian burials elsewhere has proven a far greater challenge, especially in East Anglia.

Perhaps the best known is the apparent double burial of a man and woman, whose grave was discovered at Santon near Thetford in Norfolk in 1867, on the slope of a hill to the north of the church. Sadly, our knowledge of this burial is only sketchy and nothing but the metalwork survives. This is interesting, however, as the woman had been buried with a pair of oval brooches (Fig. 15). These were originally worn to fasten the shoulder of an overdress and were a type worn by Scandinavian women from the ninth- to mid-tenth centuries. They could vary in their elaboration from crudely-cast examples to finer ones with 'double shells', an ornate outer shell overlying a simple inner one. The Santon examples are of this more expensive variety, further elaborated with twisted silver wire inlays. The man had been buried with a sword, another traditionally expensive weapon, suggesting that the pair had been of high status in life.

▽ Fig. 16

The necklace from the Viking burial excavated at Saffron Walden, Essex. Compare the design of the outer silver pendants with the 'Borre' brooches in Figs 36 and 37.
© Saffron Walden Museum.

Until recently, the only other more certain burial of a Scandinavian was also discovered in the nineteenth century, in a grave in Saffron Walden (Fig. 16). The grave was discovered in 1876 within a wider cemetery, the skeleton being buried with a knife (now lost) and an elaborate necklace comprising a pair of glass and a pair of crystal beads, framing an arrangement of two silver-gilt pendants with 'Borre' style knotwork decoration made about 900AD, a pair of carnelian beads and an elaborate central silver pendant with two silver suspension beads. Again, the grouping suggests a woman of high status. Together, these burials could be argued to represent exactly the sort of Viking dead we might expect if there were low numbers of Scandinavians settling as part of an elite takeover of East Anglia. These rare burials were apparently of wealthier people, rather than a mass-migration of ordinary Scandinavian men and women.

However, although still rare, more graves have emerged. As an example, in 1983 a burial was excavated at Middle Harling, again dating to the late ninth or early tenth century (Fig. 17). It was again accompanied by grave-goods, in this case a modest assortment of three knives, two of a pivoting-blade type, a small whetstone, an iron spur, buckles and a toilet implement (an ear scoop). Unlike the previous two burials, this grave was accurately recorded and while positioned on its own, was to the edge of an existing churchyard. Indeed, it had been dug into a ditch which may have marked the cemetery's northern boundary – in other words, this Scandinavian had been buried where dead people in the Anglo-Saxon world were buried: a churchyard, but on its very edge, alone and almost outside.

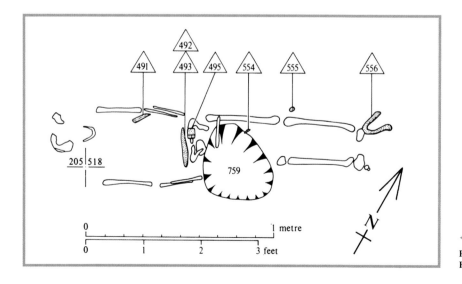

◀ Fig. 17

PLAN OF THE VIKING BURIAL EXCAVATED IN MIDDLE HARLING, NORFOLK. *DRAWING BY STEVEN ASHLEY.*

Another Viking burial was excavated in Thetford, in July 1953 to the west of the Bury Road, buried on a north-west to south-east orientation, unlike the normal Christian east-west burial tradition. The burial was accompanied on its left-hand side by an iron sword and, judging by the date of the sword, was of late ninth or early tenth-century date (Fig. 18). Once again, the body is likely to have been close to a churchyard as other Christian-burial style bodies were recovered nearby in the 1950s and 1960s. Interestingly, another body in this general area – sadly the details are unclear – seems to have been accompanied by an iron spearhead and a knife and thus was possibly another Viking buried with his weapon. Finally, and more speculatively, a burial from the Anglo-Saxon cemetery excavated at the Roman shore fort at Caister was found to have a penny of King Ecgberht of Wessex (minted in Canterbury between 828-839 although circulating into the 850s), buried under its head. This would be very unusual for a Christian, and it is suggested as more likely to be the burial of a Scandinavian. Although there are no other definite or probable Scandinavian burials from the East Anglian kingdom currently known, there is one other possible Viking grave nearby, from Wicken Fen in Cambridgeshire. There, an isolated burial was found accompanied by two knives, one of them a Late Anglo-Saxon *seax* or long fighting knife.

The burials that have been found are interesting for several reasons. First, their sheer rarity seems to say something about the lack of huge numbers of Vikings living in the kingdom and wanting to be buried in a traditional Scandinavian way. They may have accomodated quickly to local, Christian practice. Instead, the graves of those who chose to be buried with objects were often placed at the edges of churchyards as though hedging their bets with the local Christians' religion. Alternatively, they may have been tacitly accepting their social geography, of where it was right or appropriate to bury the dead. While some, perhaps particularly among the first generation of Vikings in England, may have felt little bond with the people and landscape they found, it must have been quite hard for those subsequently settling within that countryside to completely ignore the way of life they found, including using existing cemeteries, to which churches were increasingly attached. Second, those burials that have been found include two of wealthy women whose social status was projected by the jewellery they wore – jewellery which also signalled a Scandinavian identity. It suggests that this identity remained an important statement that was being made in death, and that their role or presence in wider East Anglian society was being marked. Finally, the distribution of the burials is possibly significant. With so few known, there is little clear patterning, but it may not be coincidence that they cluster around Thetford. Once again, if this was the centre of operations for the Viking army when it overwintered and fought Eadmund, it might not be so surprising to see Scandinavian individuals being buried in or near the town.

FIG. 18 ▶
Sword found in the probable Viking burial from Thetford.

EVIDENCE FOR VIKING RELIGION

If burials provide one insight into the presence of Viking beliefs and traditions, direct evidence for their religious convictions is increasingly emerging through new finds of metalwork. The most obvious of these is the Thor's hammer. According to Icelandic writer Snorri Sturlusson, Thor ranked second in the Scandinavian pantheon only after Odin, but was the 'strongest of all the gods and men'. He was associated with thunder and lightning, but is particularly well recognised for his hammer, called Mjöllnir, with which he struck down his enemies. The practice of using miniature hammers as amuletic pendants appears to have developed in Scandinavia in the ninth century, an appearance that some suggest was influenced by the Vikings seeing the Christian population of Europe wearing cross pendants. Their appearance in England is a clear sign of Vikings, as Thor's hammers were so clearly non-Christian that none would have ever been worn by a native Anglo-Saxon. Their presence therefore speaks of ethnic Scandinavians – whether raiders or subsequent immigrant settlers – bringing with them objects and ideas that were clearly un-English.

Although the number of Thor's hammers known is still not huge, this perhaps reflects the fact they were not worn by every Viking to walk the soil of England, let alone be dropped and lost by them. However, it is interesting to note that eleven have now been found in the kingdom of East Anglia, ten from Norfolk (Fig. 19), and a silver example from Sibton in Suffolk (Fig. 20). Of the ten from Norfolk, four are made of lead, perhaps a reflection of their cheap nature and

▲ Fig. 19

Six Thor's hammers of lead, silver and gold from Norfolk.

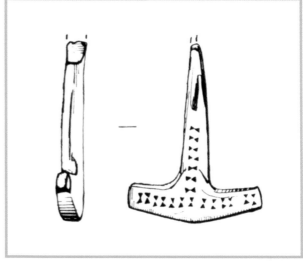

▲ Fig. 20

Silver Thor's hammer from Sibton in Suffolk, decorated with typical Viking punch–stamp decoration. © *Suffolk County Council*.

thus availability to lower levels of society. Most often, Thor's hammers are made of silver, a colour which of course any freshly-cast lead hammer would have had. Of those silver examples, decoration has sometimes been applied in the form of geometrical punch-stamp patterns, as with the examples from Sibton and South Lopham in Norfolk. The most ostentatious case is a hammer from Great Witchingham, where the head has been inlaid with a panel containing gold filigree wire (Fig. 21). Frustratingly, another silver hammer with a gold wire inlay is also supposed to have been found in Norfolk, but was never reported to archaeologists. If it was indeed from the county, it could suggest that these highly unusual examples were actually made in the kingdom rather than imported from Scandinavia. In turn, this might suggest that not only were such unchristian objects being worn and lost in Norfolk, but that there was a sufficient pagan clientele here for a workshop to be making such ornate pieces.

While Thor's hammers have been well recognised, other examples of Viking metalwork referencing non-Christian religious or mythological scenes have also been found, with direct parallels known from ninth- and tenth-century Scandinavia. One of these shows a scene of a warrior mounted on a horse being greeted by a female carrying a shield and presenting the warrior with a drinking horn or cup. Beneath the horse is a chequered panel, probably representing a gaming board. Examples have been found in Bylaugh, Norfolk (Fig. 22) and from the Peterborough area (Fig. 23). Similar examples have been found in Scandinavia, for instance one from Lake Tissø in Denmark. A second standardised depiction is of a female with a trailing skirt bearing a shield and either a spear or sword. A

▲ FIG. 22
VALKYRIE MOUNT FROM BYLAUGH, NORFOLK.

▲ FIG. 23
VALKYRIE MOUNT FROM THE PETERBOROUGH AREA.
© THE TRUSTEES OF THE BRITISH MUSEUM.

silver example has been found in Wickham Market, Suffolk (Fig. 24), while others are known from Donington, Lincolnshire and Exton in Rutland. Again, there are similar examples from Scandinavia, and they are generally interpreted as representing Valkyries, Odin's handmaidens who allotted victory on the battlefield and chose slain warriors to join him in Valhalla. Finally, a fragment of another figure with a possible moustache and tied-up hair, found in Colkirk, Norfolk, may represent another mythological character of Scandinavian tradition (Fig. 25).

It is notable that all these objects with mythological figures have been found in eastern counties of England; while the Thor's hammers are more widely spread, they also cluster most impressively on Norfolk (Fig. 26). At one level this concentration could be explained by them overwhelmingly being metal-detected finds, and Norfolk, Suffolk and Lincolnshire have a longer history of recording such finds. However, with the recording of finds now extending across England over an ever longer timespan, these distributions still hold true. At a basic level it shows their presence in the Danelaw area of England, as we might expect. However, it also hints that there was a particular favouring of such religious items in the kingdom of East Anglia. Exactly why is unclear, but once again it suggests the presence of a larger immigrant population settling down and bringing with them metalwork that was unashamedly showing their pagan beliefs.

▲ Fig. 24

Valkyrie figure from Wickham Market, Suffolk. © Colchester and Ipswich Museums, Ipswich Borough Collection, IPSMG: R.2003.12.

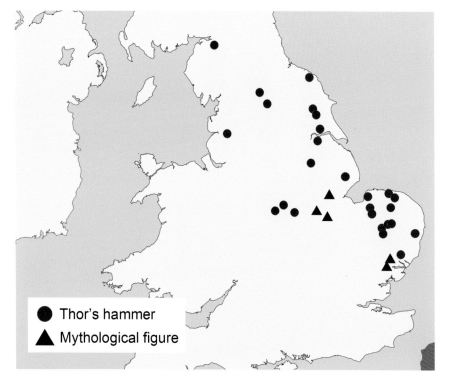

● Thor's hammer
▲ Mythological figure

▲ Fig. 25

Possible Viking-period mythological figure from Colkirk, Norfolk.

◀ Fig. 26

Distribution map of Thor's hammers and mythological figures.

Strong evidence for the conversion of the pagan Viking peoples to Christianity is suggested by the St Edmund memorial coinage. While Guthrum had been forced to convert following his defeat by Alfred of Wessex, genuine and widespread adoption of Christianity among the Viking settlers must have taken longer, not least as there was continued conflict between the West Saxons and Danelaw Vikings, where any nominal conversion might have been rejected. New arrivals are also likely to have continued appearing from the Scandinavian homelands into the 920s, bringing with them their pagan faith. The memorial coinage is therefore a clear statement by the East Anglian leadership that they were aligning themselves with a Christian cult, and therefore promoting the Christian faith.

One object that provides a fascinating possible insight into this process is a lead *bulla* or seal of Pope John XI (931-35) (Figs. A&B). Seals were used on ancient letters to show that they had either been unopened or, more important, that they were genuine correspondence from the sender that had not been tampered with. Papal documents were verified by the lead pendant seal or bulla that was attached to a string threaded through the document. The use of lead rather than wax was because papal seals had been inspired by the lead seals used for correspondence in the Byzantine imperial court and this tradition had been maintained (and in fact continued to be throughout the

 FIG. A
OBVERSE

▲ **FIG. B**
REVERSE

medieval period). The design follows those of other popes at this time, having John's name ('IOHANNIS') around an eight-pointed star on one side, and his title +PAPA ('Father' from which comes 'Pope').

There is precious little evidence for the conversion of the Vikings after their settlement, the most often mentioned being a letter written by Pope Formosus (891-6) to the bishops of England. In this he states

> Having heard that the abominable rites of the pagans have sprouted again in your parts [we pray] that you may persevere in what has been well begun [the conversion of the Vikings]. … and do not any longer in your country suffer the Christian faith to be violated.

Following the Viking invasions we have no bishop known in East Anglia until Theodred – actually the Bishop of London, but clearly acting in the kingdom until c.951. The first true post-Viking East Anglian bishop is recorded as being Eadwulf, in charge of a unified see at Elmham, who was appointed some time before 955. Given all this, the discovery of a papal bulla is interesting as well as extremely rare, as only four Anglo-Saxon period papal bullae are known from England. This example was found in Kilverstone by a metal-detectorist and suggests that by the mid-930s, when King Æthelstan was extending his rule into East Anglia, a papal document was circulating in the region. Although we have no idea what that was concerned with, its sheer existence is a sign that the Church here was now organised enough to be receiving correspondence from Rome. It is also interesting that the find-spot, Kilverstone, is just outside Thetford and at the conquest in 1066 was held by Archbishop Stigand, so may have been an episcopal estate at an earlier date. This may again point to the importance of that town in the political and religious life of tenth-century East Anglia.

A QUESTION OF STYLE:
VIKING JEWELLERY AND FASHION

If the evidence we have seen from place-names and items showing Scandinavian religious beliefs can be accepted as suggesting that Vikings and their families came to settle in some numbers in the kingdom of East Anglia, we should be unsurprised that there is an increasing amount of other metalwork that supports their presence. This comes in two principal forms: first, the sorts of jewellery we also see being made and worn at this date in Scandinavia; and second, the use of the latest fashionable art styles or designs in use there being imported into England. Some examples are so uncommon and purely Scandinavian that they can only have been produced in the Viking homelands and brought across to England. An especially ornate example is the silver-gilt pendant found in Little Snoring, Norfolk (Fig. 27). Made in the Scandinavian 'Borre' style, with so-called gripping-beast decoration, it is very similar to another pendant recovered from the Värby Hoard in Sweden, buried c.940.

FIG. 27 ▶

SILVER PENDANT FROM LITTLE SNORING, NORFOLK,
WITH TRACES OF GILDING AND NIELLO INLAY.
© THE TRUSTEES OF THE BRITISH MUSEUM.

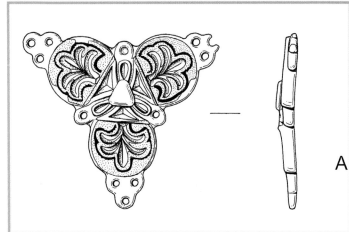

▲ Fig. 28
CAROLINGIAN TREFOIL MOUNT FROM GREAT
BARTON, SUFFOLK.
© SUFFOLK COUNTY COUNCIL.

As ever, there are various problems surrounding how we can interpret these finds. At their most basic, they revolve around how people use such objects and the ways in which style and fashion travel. It will be apparent that not everyone walking the streets of an English town and wearing a baseball cap will be American; by the same token, not every woman wearing a Scandinavian style of brooch need have been a Viking settler. Equally, the fact that such types of brooch were in common use demonstrates their popularity and the social and cultural influences that must have lain behind their widespread adoption. In short, it suggests a strong enough Scandinavian influence for their jewellery to be used and copied by those living in England.

There are a number of pieces of jewellery, typically brooches, that illustrate this especially clearly. The most distinctive of these are oval brooches of the type found in the burial at Santon (Fig. 15). Fragments of other possible oval brooches have also been found at Wormegay, Mileham and Mautby in Norfolk, but generally this type of brooch appears to be a less common form of Viking brooch from Eastern England and to have more of a distribution in northern England, for instance a pair from a female grave in a small cemetery of Scandinavians excavated at Cumwhitton in Cumbria.

However, they attest to a very different form of dress being worn by a number of women in England and this is apparent from a second distinctively different form of Scandinavian brooch, the trefoil. Comprising three lobes, these brooches were ultimately derived from Carolingian trefoil-shaped sword-belt fittings, an example of which was found in Great Barton, Suffolk (Fig. 28). Such belt fittings were taken back to Scandinavia as a result of raiding and trading in the ninth century and, like many other pieces of imported metalwork, in Scandinavian hands were converted from their original use into jewellery. This presumably gave a highly-visible and exotic show of wealth to their wearer. These trefoil-shaped pieces seem to have been particularly desirable because soon they were being widely produced as purpose-made brooches with copies of the Carolingian styles of decoration or copied in more stylised ways, or replaced with native Scandinavian motifs. Just as the Vikings produced their own versions in Scandinavia, so they brought them to England as they campaigned and settled, and a number of examples from East Anglia seem to reflect this. For instance, an elaborate moulded example with scroll ornaments was found in Colton, Norfolk (Fig. 29), while another with scrolls and animal heads at the points of the central triangle, was found at Lakenheath Warren, Suffolk. This is especially interesting as its reverse has not only the lug for its pin and a catch-plate, but a third attachment loop, which is a typically

Fig. 29 ▶

Trefoil brooch from Colton, Norfolk.

Scandinavian arrangement. A third trefoil brooch, found in Hindringham and using a more simple Scandinavian style (Fig. 30), also has these three attachment points, suggesting it was made by Scandinavian metalworkers and imported into East Anglia. Despite these examples, the most numerous form of trefoil brooch found in East Anglia is of a smaller size, with a far more stylised pattern of a 'fir-tree' design, which is actually a very stylised version of the acanthus foliage decoration seen on the larger, more finely modelled, trefoils. These are possibly a second-generation of trefoil brooches, although not simply an Anglo-Scandinavian hybrid, as a similar number of examples is also known from Scandinavia, especially Viking Age Denmark.

The close links between the production of brooches in England and Denmark seems to be shown by one sub-group of such trefoil brooches, where a design irregularity (one of the lobes being mis-aligned) is seen in both countries. The English versions have 'Anglo-Scandinavian' fittings on the reverse, being a mix of the Scandinavian pin-lug form and Anglo-Saxon catch-plate, which shows they were made in England. The use of an imported Danish brooch to create a mould, to make new examples is suggested; the brooch front would then appear to be fully Scandinavian in their design, and would have allowed the latest imports – and fashion – to have been easily replicated and worn in East Anglia and beyond. We therefore seem to see the adoption of Carolingian sword baldrics to reuse as an exotic form of jewellery showing status. The purpose-made large trefoil brooches perhaps reflect this popularity rolling out across Scandinavia and being followed by smaller and simpler types which circulated both there and in England too.

▼ FIG. 30

TREFOIL BROOCH FROM HINDRINGHAM, NORFOLK. NOTE THE THIRD ATTACHMENT POINT AT BOTTOM LEFT, AND HOW THE PIN MUST ORIGINALLY HAVE BEEN BENT.

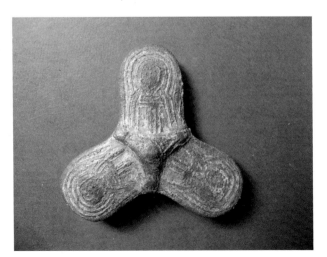

FIG. 31 ▶

GOLD LOZENGE BROOCH FROM
ATTLEBOROUGH, NORFOLK.

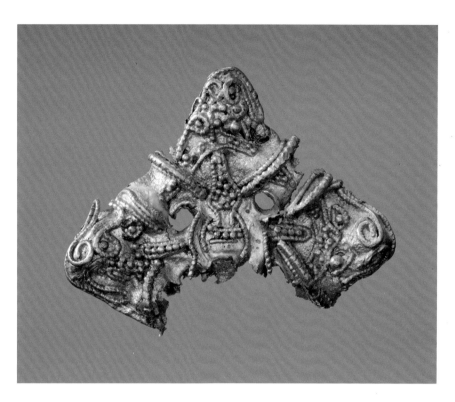

▲ FIG. 32

COPPER-ALLOY LOZENGE BROOCH
FROM WIVETON, NORFOLK. NOTE THE
ASYMMETRICAL SHAPE WITH THE SLIGHTLY
LONGER BOTTOM ARM.

Another popular brooch type helps to show this process of high-class examples having mass-produced derivatives. This is the lozenge-shaped brooch, a type which emerged in Scandinavia in the ninth century. It featured an equal-armed cross-shape, each arm ending in an outward-looking beast's head, modelled in the Borre art style. Behind the animal heads, ridges span out to join those from the adjacent heads, forming an outer edge creating the lozenge. This basic design of four outward-facing beasts was popular in the Viking world and it was perhaps natural that it should be used on brooches. A spectacular example of this was found by a metal-detectorist, torn up into four pieces, in 2013 in a field in Attleborough, Norfolk (Fig. 31). Although missing one arm, the hollow brooch (now reconstructed) was made from two sheets of gold, the upper half moulded to shape and decorated with filigree gold wire. Each animal head has a border of twisted wire and the eyes are formed by single gold granules surrounded by a circle of beaded wire. Perhaps equally important, the four cruciform arms that form the centre of the design are formed from a thick granulated wire flanked by thinner twisted wires.

The presence of such a magnificent gold brooch in Norfolk points to an owner of some status and wealth, and suggests that the object had been imported into East Anglia, where such gold and filigree-decorated jewellery was not the norm. The use of four beasts' heads on a mount is known from a gold and filigree pendant found in the large hoard from Hoen in Norway, dating from the ninth century. Such brooches must have formed the inspiration for the many, slightly smaller, copper-alloy lozenge brooches that have been found in England and southern Scandinavia, and which enabled a mass-market to own and wear similar examples (Fig. 32). The design of these was clearly imitating the precious gold examples, several of which, despite being of a gold colour when freshly-made out of brass or bronze, were additionally gilded. Moreover, the decoration of the central cross-arms uses beading to imitate the gold wire.

Once again, we can see from the frequency of such lozenge brooches appearing in East Anglia, that the fashion for items popular in Scandinavia made its way over to England too. Moreover, this was satisfied by their production locally. One group of lozenge brooches has been identified with a common design in which one of the animal-headed terminals is slightly longer than the others, creating an unbalanced shape. This suggests that they derive from a defective model originally used to make the moulds. Their distribution in the area around Norwich suggests that they may have been produced in the early town there.

While I have focused on three particular brooch types, one of the interesting features of Viking Age East Anglia is just how many different, yet standardised, brooch types and designs there were, using different styles of Scandinavian art and with similar examples also found in the Viking homelands. For instance, 'convex disc brooches', typically about two and a half to three and a half centimetres in diameter, were clearly popular and a number have similar designs. One, in the Scandinavian 'Borre' style, has an almost whimsical device of three animal heads looking inwards and resting their noses at the high point in the brooch's centre (Fig. 33). This brooch type has once again been found in Scandinavia, with a widespread distribution but particular concentrations in the south and east of Sweden, for instance the Uppland region, Gotland and Birka, as well as Uppåkra and Hedeby in the Danish kingdom. Although in England their distribution extends from Suffolk up to Yorkshire, perhaps interestingly, the majority of this type has been found in Norfolk. Other items show different influences, a strap-end later converted into a brooch having 'ring-chain' ornament seen in tenth-century Borre and Jelling art (Fig. 34). A panel of ring-chain appears on an especially charming animal-head fitting from North Creake which, from the hole in its neck, was possibly attached to a chain (Fig. 35).

▲ FIG. 33
GILDED BORRE CONVEX BROOCH FROM BURNHAM MARKET, NORFOLK.

▲ FIG. 34
COPPER-ALLOY STRAP-END FROM CONGHAM, NORFOLK, ORNAMENTED WITH BORRE RING-CHAIN DECORATION.

We need to be slightly cautious as Norfolk in particular has an outstanding record of recording metal-detector finds, which means that it often features numerically more examples of any given find-type. However, the dense concentration, as well as the sheer variety of brooch-types that were evidently available, suggests this was a genuine preference. This is backed up by some examples having Anglo-Saxon types of pin-fitting on the reverse, showing that they were indeed being made in East Anglia. If a conscious decision was apparently being made by customers to choose this design of brooch within Norfolk especially, we can explore this further by looking at two more types of disc brooch, one featuring a knotwork device, the other a beast looking backwards over its shoulder. Unlike the various convex-type brooches, these are flat-faced and larger and, throughout, use Anglo-Saxon pin arrangements on the reverse showing them to be an English product.

▽ Fig. 35

RING-CHAIN ORNAMENTED ANIMAL-HEAD
TERMINAL FROM NORTH CREAKE, NORFOLK.

VIKING PLAQUES AND LINEN SMOOTHERS

In contrast to the emphasis on Viking raiding and warbands roaming the countryside, archaeological excavations have helped to demonstrate the trading and domestic aspect to Scandinavian settlement. In many cases it can be difficult to see a particular difference between Anglo-Saxon and Viking people as they all used the same types of pottery (in East Anglia of Thetford Ware: Fig. 52), lived in similar houses and ate the same foods.

◀ Fig. A
The whalebone plaque from Stuntney near Ely.
© University of Cambridge Museum of
Archaeology & Anthropology (1922.895 A).

However, there are sometimes finds that are more distinctively Scandinavian, for instance the whalebone plaque that was found near Stuntney, Ely in the early twentieth century (Fig. A). These plaques or boards are commonly found in northern Norway and have been conventionally interpreted as smoothing-boards used for pressing out seams and pleats. While some have more recently suggested that they may have been chopping boards or food-trays, they were clearly objects associated with a degree of status in the Viking world, and usually found in rich female graves, presumably associated with the woman's role in running the household.

While the plaques are quite rare items, if they were indeed used for the treatment of textiles, it might be that they were originally more common in wood and therefore have not survived. Their counterpart in the process, 'linen smoothers', have not only been found in Viking female graves but in excavations, such as in Norwich and Thetford (Fig. B). Made of thick, rounded, bun-shaped, pieces of glass, they have a central depression on the underside and would be smooth enough to rub the linen without catching on threads. Once again, they attest to Scandinavian types of object being introduced into England, most probably with female immigrants, and show an aspect of day-to-day practices rather than just fashion or style shown in jewellery through brooches. This creates another strand in showing the increasing presence of Scandinavian people arriving in East Anglia.

FIG. B ▶

LINEN SMOOTHERS FROM EXCAVATIONS
IN NORWICH AND THETFORD.

EAST ANGLIAN BROOCHES – A REGIONAL IDENTITY?

The first brooch type, of the knotwork design, seems to trace its origins to Scandinavia, with pendants and especially brooches developing from designs mainly seen in Denmark in the late ninth or early tenth centuries. An example of such a pendant comes from the Saffron Walden burial (Fig. 16). In East Anglia, the design became incredibly popular with just two main variants: with a central circular depression (Fig. 36); or one in which the central circle was better defined by a circular band that highlighted the surrounding tendril decoration (Fig. 37). The second brooch type features an almost identically-sized disc with identical pin arrangements on the reverse. The four-legged animal is sometimes shown with paw-like toes and always has its head to the left, with a mane running down the left edge of the brooch. Its snout fills the space above its back and its eye is formed from a large ring-and-dot, with a spiky tail pointing up (Fig. 38). These charming animals seem to have a ninth-century origin, quite possibly in East Anglia.

What is most significant about these two brooch types is just how common they are in East Anglia; while examples have been found further afield, most notably in Lincolnshire and Yorkshire, East Anglia was clearly their home (Figs 39 and 40). The numbers are impressive, with over 230 knotwork brooches alone known. Equally important is the number of them relative to the other types of Viking Age brooches known – one scholar noted the knotwork brooches to represent 47% of all Scandinavian and Anglo-Scandinavian brooches in England, while another noted the 'beast' brooches to be 40% of all Anglo-Scandinavian brooches in Norfolk. That means that not only were these two brooch types overwhelmingly common, despite the wide variety of types and designs of other brooches that were available in the tenth century, but that they were exceedingly *popular*. Why?

If we accept that most of the Viking brooches were as easy as each other to make, their ease of manufacture and associated cost should not be an issue. That means the designs on the knotwork and beast brooches were particularly favoured despite being, to all intents and purposes, just as 'useful' or decorative. Clearly these two designs meant something to the wearers in their sheer uniformity, which in turn suggests some form of deeper shared identity, with people wanting to dress in a similar way. Exactly why this was important to the East Anglian inhabitants is difficult to say, but historically groups of people faced by external threats or differences have tended to respond with expressions of similarity to reflect their shared identity. This can take various forms, such as of language spoken, religion practiced or styles of dress. Dating the brooches accurately within the tenth century, which might

▲ FIG. 36
BORRE KNOTWORK BROOCH WITH PRONOUNCED CIRCULAR DEPRESSION, FROM AN EXCAVATION AT ANGLIA TV IN NORWICH.

▲ FIG. 37
BORRE KNOTWORK BROOCH WITH TENDRIL DECORATION AND A SEPARATE CIRCULAR CENTRE, AGAIN FROM THE ANGLIA TV EXCAVATIONS IN NORWICH.

▲ FIG. 38
BACKWARD-FACING BEAST BROOCH FROM BURGH CASTLE, NORFOLK.

help us to understand a possible stimulus for such moves, is difficult as nearly all have been found by metal-detectorists and therefore loose in the ploughsoil rather than in closely datable archaeological layers. The likelihood is that they are from the first half of the tenth century. Rather than pointing to an exact moment in time, they do nonetheless appear when the historic kingdom of East Anglia was undergoing an important and quite possibly traumatic change as the Scandinavian element of the population – by now second and third-generation immigrant descendants – and the Anglo-Saxon East Anglian population were forming a new Anglo-Scandinavian people. While the two brooch types could be seen as representing internally-divided 'Scandinavian' and 'East Anglian' factions, the similarity of the brooches suggest they should be regarded as essentially the same type. Against this backdrop, the West Saxon kings under King Alfred's son Edward the Elder and his grandson Æthelstan, were conquering and absorbing former Danelaw areas like East Anglia into a new, larger, kingdom – England. Many in East Anglia may have been less than happy to have these new outsiders, and it may be that there was at this time an 'East-Anglo-Scandinavian' identity, witnessed in part by the popularity of such local jewellery types.

▲ Fig. 39

Distribution of Borre knotwork brooches.

▲ Fig. 40

Distribution of 'backward-facing beast' brooches.

TRADERS AND RAIDERS

If the Vikings are known for one activity above all others, it is raiding. However, it has become increasingly recognised they were also great traders, with their nautical know-how enabling them to carry commodities over great distances. Nevertheless, as historian Eric John once pointed out: 'The Mafia owns launderettes, hotels, restaurants and pizza parlours, but that does not make them legitimate businessmen, i.e. traders'. The truth is, both elements were often part of the same process as, for instance, men and women seized in raiding might be shipped abroad and sold as slaves as easily as gold and silver. Likewise, raiding and slavery had been endemic among the Anglo-Saxon kingdoms before a Viking ever set foot in England. What was distinctively different about the Vikings was the sheer scale and ferocity of their raids, as frightening and far-reaching as Blitzkrieg was in 1940. Finding evidence of the trading and raiding is something finally being revealed and understood, largely as a result of finds made through metal-detecting in England.

Unlike the Anglo-Saxons, or in the Carolingian empire of the Continent, the Vikings did not use coinage. Instead, they used precious-metal bullion – overwhelmingly of silver – as a medium of exchange. Their interest in coinage therefore extended only so far as considering its purity. To gauge this, coins

◀ Fig. 41
THE CUERDALE HOARD.
© THE TRUSTEES OF THE BRITISH MUSEUM.

were frequently bent or nicked with a knife, a process called 'pecking', as the softer the metal, the greater its silver purity. Likewise, silver jewellery was seen as a portable store of wealth as much as an artistic statement, and was often chopped up to be used as 'hacksilver' bullion. A wonderful portrait of this comes from Snorri Sturluson's *Heimskringla*, describing how the poet Eyvind was paid for making up a long poem about the Icelanders:

Every free farmer gave him a penny in tribute … and when the silver was paid in at the Althingi, they arranged for a smith to refine it. The silver was fashioned into a cloak-pin, less the cost of the craftsman's fee. The pin weighed 50 marks. They sent it to Eyvind. He had the pin chopped into hack-silver and with it bought himself livestock.

▼ Fig. 42
The Vale of York Hoard, found near Harrogate.
© The Trustees of the British Museum.

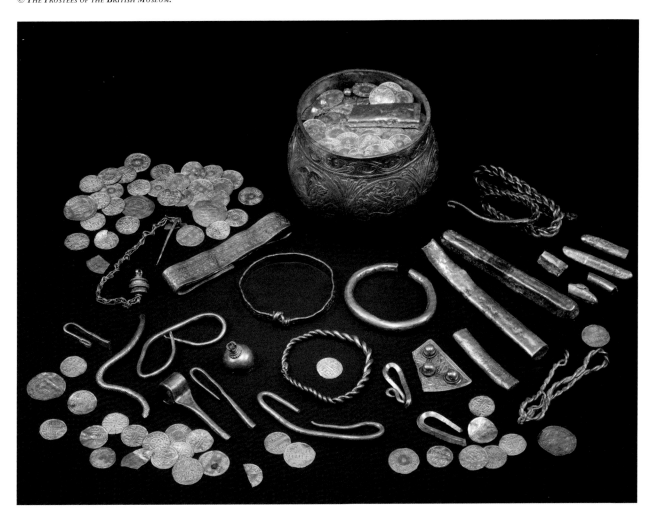

Finally, coins and jewellery might be melted down and cast as ingots which might themselves be chopped up to provide smaller quantities of silver.

The appearance of this bullion economy seems to date to the mid-ninth century, as it is about then that such finds begin to appear in Scandinavia at sites like Hedeby then in Denmark and Kaupang in Norway, and soon after in England at places like Torksey in Lincolnshire, where a Viking overwintering camp was established in 872-3. Its use in England is seen most famously in the Cuerdale Hoard, a massive store of Viking wealth unearthed on the banks of the river Ribble in Lancashire in 1840. Buried sometime between 905-10, it comprised over 40 kilos of silver, including at least 8,500 pieces of silver and over 7,500 coins (Fig. 41). Metal-detection in particular is beginning to show just how intense this bullion economy was in the north of England, with new

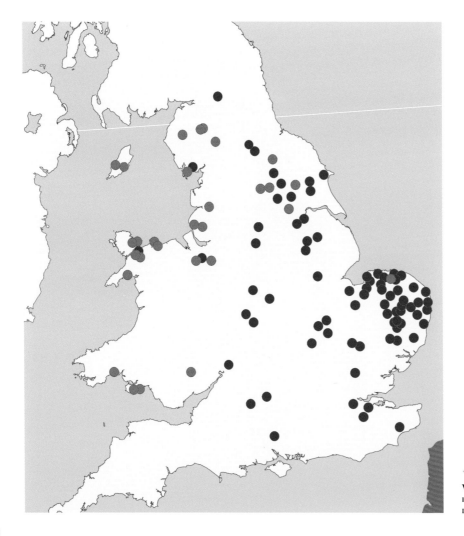

◀ FIG. 43

VIKING INGOTS FROM BRITAIN. RED DOTS INDICATE INGOTS FOUND IN HOARDS, BLUE DOTS INDIVIDUAL INGOT FINDS.

hoards appearing annually, most remarkably those from Bedale in 2012 and the 'Vale of York' hoard found near Harrogate in 2007 (Fig. 42).

Interestingly, despite its clear Scandinavian occupation, East Anglia is more like the rest of southern England in seeing largely a continuation of coin-use, with the Viking rulers – as we have seen – swiftly coming to strike coins memorialising Saint Edmund. Nevertheless, there is good evidence for the Scandinavian use of bullion running alongside that of coinage, a process called the 'dual economy'. Had we had the evidence of hoards alone, the dual economy would be seen as a far more localised feature of the north, and associated with the Hiberno-Norse sphere of influence there, which linked the Viking stronghold cities of York and Dublin. Instead, once again, responsible metal-detecting is helping to rewrite our knowledge of the situation, and East Anglia features very clearly in this (Fig. 43), as single finds of ingots are relatively common, and in one case a modest hoard of four silver ingots has been found in Hindringham (Fig. 44).

It is interesting to think about the relative values of these ingots. While there are contemporary coin hoards of this date from East Anglia, for instance the Morley St Peter hoard of 883 pennies buried *c*.924, 'purse-hoards' (small coin hoards) are actually quite rare. Yet, the loss of an ingot can represent the value of many such hoards. For instance, a single silver ingot found in Old Buckenham weighs 62.38g, equivalent to over 44 Viking Age pennies (Fig. 45).

FIG. 44 ▶

THE SILVER INGOT HOARD FROM HINDRINGHAM, NORFOLK.

FIG. 45

SILVER INGOT WITH TYPICAL VIKING 'TRANSVERSE HAMMERING' ON THE TOP, FROM OLD BUCKENHAM, NORFOLK.

The hoard of four ingots from Hindringham weighs a combined 94.08g or 83.02g of pure silver – or over 58 pennies, which would rate it as one of the largest ninth- or tenth-century silver coin hoards found in the East Anglian kingdom. These stray-finds of isolated silver ingots therefore represent serious losses by their owners, and reflect the value and volume of silver that must have been circulating within the region.

Another feature of the large silver hoards from the north of England has been the regular inclusion of Arabic *dirham* coins, imported from the Islamic world and brought to Scandinavia via the Russian river systems, principally by Swedish Vikings. It is true that Western Europe had enjoyed links with the Arabic world much earlier, as gold dinar coins of the eighth century show, for instance examples found in Wickhampton, Norfolk and Brandon, Suffolk (Fig. 46). There was even the celebrated diplomatic gift of an elephant named Abu l'Abbas to Charlemagne from the Abbasid Caliph, Harun Al-Rashid, in 802 (the name, disappointingly, may mean simply 'the Abbasid elephant' or a more fun alternative 'father of wrinkles'). However, it was only from the mid ninth century, and as a result of Viking exploits through Russia, that the wealth of Arabic silver was truly opened up and brought into the west.

Coming across the North Sea, dirhams came to be included in large hoards like those from the Vale of York or Cuerdale. However, metal-detection has once again shown their use in the local East Anglian economy, circulating alongside other coinage and ingots, for instance that from Bylaugh of Caliph al-Mutadid, minted in al-Shash (modern Tashkent in Uzbekistan) in 899-900AD (286AH) (Fig. 47) and another from Burnham Market of the Samanid ruler Ahmad Il Ismail. The latter is of interest as it was minted in 912-13, making it a relatively late dirham which probably didn't arrive in East Anglia

FIG. 46

ABBASID GOLD DINAR FROM WICKHAMPTON, NORFOLK, DATING FROM AH 157 (773-4 AD).

until about 920, by which time use of coinage had supposedly been restored under Edward the Elder. Moreover, four sites in Norfolk – Barton Bendish, Shipdham, Sparham and Oxborough – have yielded cut fragments, those from Barton Bendish, for instance together weighing only 1.1g, about a third of a complete dirham. As well as attesting to the skill of the detectorists who found them, these tiny pieces of hacksilver show that they were being used in even very small portions for trade or payment, just as they were in ninth- and tenth-century Scandinavia at such trading sites as Kaupang in Norway.

An important corollary of using bullion for trade and exchange was inevitably the apparatus for measuring the precious metal changing hands. For this, balances and weights were essential. The fragile copper-alloy balances used have been found as broken parts in excavations in such Viking towns as Thetford and York, but also in the countryside through metal-detecting. More common as finds have been the weights needed, and these form three basic types. Most unusual in East Anglia are those of 'octo-cubohedral' shape – essentially cubes with their corners cut off. Generally made of copper-alloy, they are better known from metal-detecting in Lincolnshire and Yorkshire. More common are a second type, of flat-ended spherical weights where an iron core was encased in a brass or bronze outer skin. These appear to have been derived from the Arabic world and some examples even seem to copy a pseudo-arabic inscription at one end. Finally, many weights are a simple conical, squared or drum shaped block of lead, definable as Viking from

▲ Fig. 47

SILVER DIRHAM FOUND IN BYLAUGH, NORFOLK.

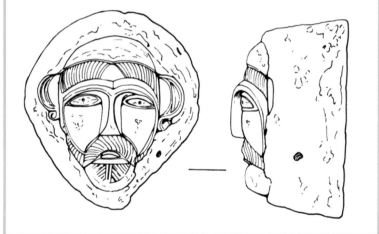

▲ Fig. 48

LEAD VIKING WEIGHT FROM IXWORTH, SUFFOLK, WITH AN INLAID HEAD OF INSULAR MANUFACTURE. *Photo © West Suffolk Heritage Services; line drawing © Suffolk County Council.*

the metalwork or occasionally base metal coins like the 'stycas' used in the
Northumbrian kingdom, set into the top.

Some examples are highly decorative, for instance the lead weight found
in Ixworth, featuring a fragment of gilt copper-alloy sheet cut down from
a larger object (Fig. 48). Showing a bearded head with a stylised fringe and
curling locks behind the ears, this seems to have been originally from an

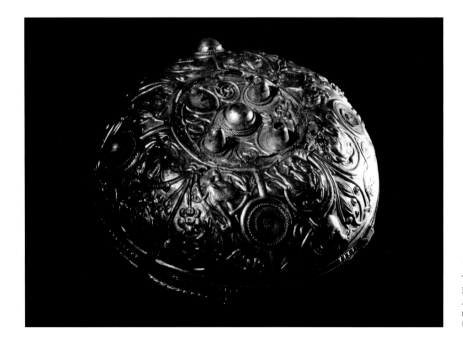

Irish object that was cut down to fit the weight. Likewise, a chopped-down fragment of small gilt silver sheet from a lead weight found at Great Ryburgh is decorated with Anglo-Saxon interlace decoration of eighth-century date (Fig. 49). One can only appreciate what type of beautiful object it may once have belonged to when looking at the base of the magnificent silver-gilt Ormside Bowl, itself probably buried with a Viking, before being discovered in the nineteenth century (Figs 50).

East Anglia does, then, have clear evidence for the same kinds of Viking trade items and bullion seen elsewhere in Viking Age England (Fig. 51). At the same time, it has never yielded the large silver bullion hoards that have been found in the north of England and Scotland. Hoards suggest that, for instance, dirhams first entered England in large numbers from the middle of the ninth century at much the same time as in Scandinavia, continuing into the early tenth century. This suggests that it was part of the same trade network. However, from *c.*925 there seems to be a decline, certainly in southern England, with Scotland and Ireland seeing such bullion hoards continuing until 950-70. With the rise of the St Edmund memorial coinage from about 915, East Anglia and its immediate Danelaw neighbours appear once again to have had more of an organised system of coinage. Our finds therefore suggest that the 'dual economy' of coinage and bullion lasted a far shorter time in the old East Anglian kingdom, although it had been fully exposed to its workings.

FIG. 51 ▶

VIKING WEIGHTS, DIRHAMS AND SILVER INGOTS, ALL
FOUND AS ISOLATED FINDS FROM SITES IN NORFOLK.

A BONE FLUTE MADE FROM THE
TARSOMETATARSUS (LOWER LEG BONE) OF
A CRANE, EXCAVATED FROM THETFORD.

Despite all the undoubted violence and danger present in the lives of many during the Viking Age, people did also take the opportunity to enjoy themselves with music, poetry and games. Although we don't know what their music actually sounded like, a number of flutes from the period have been found in excavations, made of the wing and leg bones of cranes and swans, with finger and thumb holes much like a modern recorder (Fig. A). The popularity of poetry and stories quite probably lent themselves to musical interludes or backing, as well as for dancing or generally listening to.

Board games were also very popular and it is clear that the ability to play them was considered a skill that any 'gentleman' Viking should have. In a poem in the *Orkneyinga Saga*, Rognvald Kali, later an earl of Orkney, describes the first of his

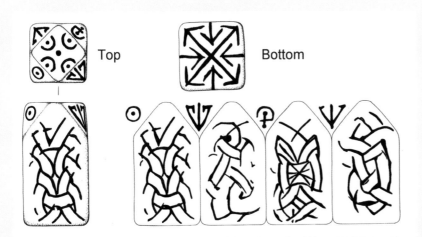

▲ FIG. B

LINE DRAWING OF ALL SIX FACES OF THE BAWDSEY GAMING PIECE. © *SUFFOLK COUNTY COUNCIL*.

▲ FIG. C

NINETEENTH-CENTURY ENGRAVING OF THE THELTON GAMING PIECE.

nine accomplishments as 'artful I am at *tafl*'. *Tafl*, also known as *hnefatafl*, was a game in which one player occupied the centre of the board, at the very centre of which stood the king (or *hnefi*). The other player occupied the edges of the board and tried to prevent the king from reaching an edge.

A number of Viking Age playing pieces has been found in East Anglia that may well have been used for playing games like *tafl*, three of particularly fine quality. One, from Bawdsey in Suffolk, was found in 1969 and is made from jet with a squared shaft that has its corners cut off (Fig. B). It is decorated most crucially with a ring-chain interlace design, drawn from Viking art, that dates it to the tenth century. An earlier find of a jet gaming-piece was made in Thelton, Norfolk in 1866 and is an upright rectangular tapering slab with a cylindrical top and is decorated with lines and ring-and-dot designs (Fig. C). Finally, a third jet piece which is similar but with a V-shaped notch cut out of the top, was found in 1919 in Weeting, Norfolk (Fig. D). This is a square-shaped slab, and with ring-and-dots linked by incised lines.

Jet seems to have been sourced from the area of Whitby in Yorkshire at this date and was exploited principally by the Vikings. These three pieces illustrate that in the years before the arrival of chess to Britain, board-games like *tafl* could involve the use of equally stylish and showy playing pieces. It is a reminder that for all our preconceptions about the Vikings as warriors, they were equally interested in sophisticated and thoughtful games of strategy.

FIG. D ▶
THE WEETING GAMING PIECE.

FROM RAIDS TO TRADE, AND OBJECTS MADE

What is interesting about this period of intense economic activity in the tenth century is that it seems to have been the stimulus for more permanent places to conduct trade. In the pre-Viking period, the kingdom of East Anglia appears to have had one pre-eminent town, Ipswich, which was the focus of international trade with large quantities of imported pottery. It had a mint, evidence of craft-working, and was a regional hub for the production of a distinctive pottery, Ipswich Ware, which was traded and used throughout East Anglia. This *emporium* may well have been linked to a power centre in the south-east of the kingdom, developed in the seventh century by a royal dynasty that was buried at Snape and Sutton Hoo, had a royal palace at Rendlesham and established their bishopric or see at a place called *Dommoc*, probably Walton Castle near Felixstowe. Regionally, markets and centres for trade seem to have been based at or near to major estates, both owned by the Church and aristocratic families. Places like Bawsey, Burnham and Caistor St Edmund in Norfolk, and Barham and Coddenham in Suffolk

◀ **Fig. 52**

THETFORD WARE POT FOUND BENEATH THE NORMAN CASTLE MOUND IN NORWICH. THE CRACKS ON THE RIM INDICATE THIS IS A DISCARDED 'KILN WASTER' WHICH DID NOT FIRE CORRECTLY — WHICH IN TURN SUGGESTS POTTERY PRODUCTION NEARBY.

have all produced large quantities of coinage that suggest a market economy dispersed across smaller centres throughout the kingdom, much like a series of small market towns.

The arrival of the Vikings seems to have proven traumatic for such undefended sites and it is likely that a response to this was for trade to become more centralised in defended settlements. This was certainly the case in the south-west of England, where the West Saxon kings established a network of *burhs* or defensible settlements to which mints, markets and administration were relocated. In East Anglia, Ipswich appears to have suffered a decline with the Viking raids, doubtless partially a result of its more exposed position, easily reached from the coast up the river Orwell.

In its place Thetford, straddling the Norfolk-Suffolk border, rose to importance. Many recent accounts stress the Vikings as responsible for the development of the town and this may well be true. Equally the distribution of coinage of such East Anglian kings as Æthelstan (*c.*825-40) and Eadmund (*c.*855-869) cluster around Thetford, suggesting that the minting of their coins may well have been transferred from Ipswich to Thetford by the 820s or 830s (Fig 7). It was also probably the reason it was to Thetford that the Vikings came to overwinter in 869, before killing Eadmund. However, they then appear to have adopted and developed the town. Perhaps the most notable example of this is that pottery production appears to have stopped in Ipswich in about 850, whereupon a new pottery type became the norm throughout East Anglia: Thetford ware (Fig. 52). That the pottery should be first identified in Thetford is probably not coincidental. Whether it owes its origins to a relocation of urban functions to Thetford by the East Anglian royal family or by the Vikings is unclear. However, it is interesting that another of the Viking overwintering camps, Torksey in Lincolnshire, also came to have a regional pottery industry established from the late ninth century.

Equally important, metal-detection at Torksey has revealed the detritus of the Viking camp in the form of coins, weights, hacksilver, ingots and dirhams. It would therefore seem that such 'camps' were more like small towns, overseeing the trade and shipment of the profit made in the campaigning season, acting as a provisioning and resupply point for the army at rest, and home to the various wives, girlfriends and children who, as we have seen, accompanied the army. In such a light, it is easy to see how a place like Thetford may, paradoxically, have received an economic boost after it became a place for overwintering Vikings in 869-70. One hint of the wealth available in the town is the fine gold finger-ring found there, typically Viking in style with a lozenge-shaped bezel with punch-stamp decoration (Fig. 53). Archaeological excavations have shown how densely occupied Thetford was by the tenth century, with a large number of churches attesting to the rapid conversion of those Vikings who had settled there.

Norwich seems to have benefitted from the increased presence of a Scandinavian population by the tenth century. While eighth-century origins are suggested from archaeology, it seems more likely that a major estate and trading site of this date stood to the south of the modern city at Caistor St Edmund, across the river Tas to the south of the walled Roman town of *Venta Icenorum*. From the ninth century on, probably aided by the broader river Wensum, settlement grew in Norwich, initially it seems as ribbon development on both banks of the river. It is in the tenth century that the first evidence emerges for the town, which was visibly vibrant and increasingly densely occupied. That this should have occurred following settlement and increasing integration of the Vikings with the Anglo-Saxon population is probably no coincidence. While political tensions continued with the extension of territorial control under the West Saxon kings into East Anglia, the ending of Viking raids must have allowed a town like Norwich with its direct river access to the coast to flourish.

Indeed, it is from this time we first hear of Norwich – the 'North Wic' – by name, the settlement now being the site of a mint and striking coins for King Æthelstan 'King of all England' (924-39) (Fig. 54). Although the north 'wic' could conceivably be a reference to a new *wic* or trading place in the north of the former kingdom - as distinct from *Gippeswic* or Ipswich in the south - it is more likely that the name for the town derives from the principal trading site lying to the north of the river Wensum. Study of the later medieval road layout had suggested to archaeologists that an enclosure lay immediately north of the river, creating a rectilinear shape. Subsequent excavations at Calvert Street on the proposed western boundary proved that a large ditch and bank had indeed once been positioned here (Fig. 55). The ditch had originally been some 2m deep and recut twice, before its defensive bank, inside (or behind) the ditch, was pushed into the ditch to level the ground in the twelfth century, a time when such an enclosure was no longer needed and the city was continuing to expand. The date of this enclosure's construction is uncertain, although a radiocarbon date suggests a tenth-century origin.

▲ Fig. 53
VIKING GOLD RING FOUND IN JUNE 1905 IN THETFORD.

▲ Fig. 54
PENNY OF ÆTHELSTAN OF ENGLAND, PRODUCED BY THE MINT OF NORWICH.

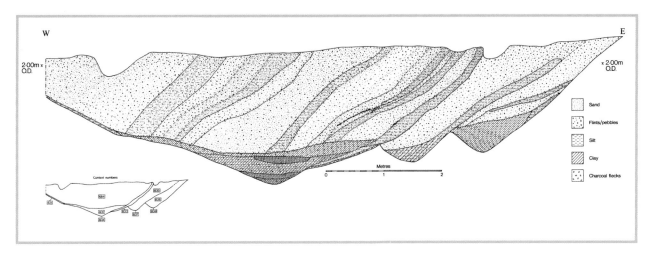

W   E

2.00m ×
O.D.   × 2.00m
                                                                                                O.D.

Context numbers

Metres
0   1   2

Sand

Flints/pebbles

Silt

Clay

Charcoal flecks

▲ Fig. 55

CROSS-SECTION DRAWING THROUGH THE
NORTH *WIC* DITCH EXCAVATED AT CALVERT
STREET, NORWICH. THIS SHOWS THAT BEFORE
BEING FILLED IN, THE DITCH HAD BEEN RECUT
TWICE, GRADUALLY CREEPING FURTHER WEST.

Similarly, a defensive earthwork found in excavations in Ipswich is suggested
to have been built in the early tenth century. However, having been the pre-
eminent town in the kingdom in the eighth and early ninth century, the rise
of Thetford and then Norwich challenged this position. Excavations at the
Buttermarket and Foundation Street show occupation becoming less dense,
with one metalled road abandoned in the later ninth century, and buildings
being set back further from the street. However, there was a ninth-century
antler-working industry making combs (Fig. 56) and continuity with Thetford
ware-type pottery being produced in the tenth century. From the end of the
century, a mint was re-established in the town.

The problem in dating these urban enclosures in Norwich and Ipswich goes to
the heart of knowing more about the political situation in the former kingdom
of East Anglia. As we have seen from the jewellery, an ethnic Scandinavian

FIG. 56 ▷

TENTH- OR ELEVENTH-CENTURY COMB
MADE OF RED DEER ANTLER EXCAVATED
FROM WHITEFRIARS STREET, NORWICH.

population had continued to keep in touch with its homelands while mixing
with the native East Anglians, adopting Christianity and coinage. This emerging
new Anglo-Scandinavian population would appear to have forged its own local
identity and in such circumstances it is not impossible that they preferred rule
by Scandinavians rather than the English West Saxon kings. Was the enclosure
in Norwich built at an earlier date, potentially as a defensive enclosure against
the West Saxon advance? Or was it perhaps part of a strategy of Æthelstan
to create a defensible enclave in a newly-captured territory, helping impose
English rule in an occupied Viking town and region, along with a new mint?
We can certainly see there was some local tension at the time. Edward the
Elder, Æthelstan's father, died in 924 and three coin hoards were buried at this
time: at Morley St Peter and Framingham Earl in Norfolk and at Brantham
in Suffolk (Fig. 57). A fourth 'purse' hoard of three coins of this date, from
Quidenham, probably reflects the fears of one person with rather less available
cash. Nevertheless, the irresistible force of the West Saxons saw the conquest
of the remainder of the Danelaw area, and ultimately brought all these
expanding towns into the newly-established English kingdom. East Anglia was
to retain its political identity in some measure by becoming an earldom, but its
cultural identity was by now distinctly Anglo-Scandinavian.

▼ Fig. 57
The Morley St Peter Hoard of
883 pennies excavated in 1958,
with the Thetford Ware pot in
which they had been hidden.

NEW RAIDS, NEW KINGS: THE SECOND VIKING AGE IN EAST ANGLIA

While the Viking raids of the eighth and ninth centuries grew from small independent war-bands, in the late tenth century new raids came to be more closely associated with Denmark, which had been transformed into a powerful, centralised, kingdom with a capacity for military organisation. The raids were typically led by the king himself, or powerful independent warlords with equally disciplined troops. The raids first began soon after King Æthelred 'the Unready' came to the throne. His epithet, *unraed*, actually meaning ill-advised, has coloured understanding of the complex politics of the time, with a population that was in many areas like East Anglia, of mixed Anglo-Scandinavian stock. Together with the factional politics that were a legacy of his father, Edgar's reign, Æthelred was to some extent a king in the wrong place at the wrong time. However, the length of his reign – 37 years – should caution against him being seen simply as a poor king.

After a gradual increase in the raiding in the 980s, a turning point in Æthelred's reign seems to have come in 991. In their first raid since 988, a

▼ FIG. 58

NORTHEY ISLAND ON WHICH THE VIKINGS LANDED BEFORE BEING ALLOWED TO CROSS THE TIDAL CAUSEWAY TO GIVE BATTLE.

Viking force under their famed Norwegian leader Olaf Tryggvason landed on Northey Island on the tidal river Blackwater next to Maldon in Essex (Fig. 58). The aged local leader, Ealdorman Byrhtnoth, who it seems had defeated a similar force at the same place three years previously, gave battle but lost and was killed in the fight. The event was memorialised in the celebrated heroic Old English poem *The Battle of Maldon*, written soon after to commemorate Byrhtnoth's heroic death with his faithful warriors:

> … so Æthelred's earl, the prince of those people
> Fell; all his hearth-companions could see
> For themselves that their lord lay low
> Then the proud thanes went forth there,
> The brave men hastened eagerly:
> They all wished, then, for one of two things –
> To avenge their lord, or to leave this world…

The *Anglo-Saxon Chronicle* was, as ever, far more brief. Recording how the Vikings had first harried Ipswich it records only 'very soon afterwards ealdorman Byrhtnoth was slain at Maldon.' More significantly it went on:

> In this year it was decided for the first time to pay tribute to the Danes because of the great terror they inspired along the sea coast. On this first occasion it amounted to ten thousand pounds.

In all, over the next 50 years the English were to pay £250,000 to the Vikings in tribute payments. The true cost to the country was even greater considering the need to raise English troops (or levies) to try and fight them, and the wholesale looting of the country. East Anglia was naturally often in the front line and in 992 it was ships raised by Æthelred from the region and from London that engaged the Danes at sea 'and they made great slaughter of them'. A particularly bad year for the region was in 1004 when King Swein Forkbeard 'came with his fleet to Norwich and completely sacked the borough and burnt it down'. The episode, recorded by the *Anglo-Saxon Chronicle* is worth quoting in full as an illustration of the Vikings using mobile tactics and the difficulties the English had in responding:

> Then Ulfcytel and the chief men from East Anglia decided that it would be better for them to buy peace from the enemy before they did too much damage in that district, since they had come unexpectedly, and he had not time to gather his levies together. However, under cover of the truce which was to have been observed between them, the host [Vikings] came up secretly from the ships and made their way to Thetford. When Ulfcytel

discovered this, he sent men to hew their ships to pieces, but those detailed for it failed in their duty, so he mobilized in secret as strong a force of levies as he could. The host reached Thetford within three weeks of sacking Norwich, and spent a night in the borough, pillaging and burning it to the ground. The next morning, when they planned to retire to their ships, Ulfcytel came up with his force so they were compelled to give battle and there was a fierce encounter and great slaughter on each side. There were slain the chief men of East Anglia, but if they had been up to full strength the enemy would never have got back to their ships, and they themselves admitted that they had never met with harder hand-play in England than Ulfcytel gave them.

Judging by the *Knútsdrápa*, a poem by Ottar the Black in praise of King Cnut, Cnut was accompanying his father, Swein Forkbeard on the Norwich raid. The composition includes the stanza:

Gracious giver of mighty gifts, you made corselets red in Norwich.
You will lose your life before your courage fails.

Six years later the Chronicle records Ulfcytel being called into action again, when a Viking army under Olaf Tryggvason landed in Ipswich

and went straightaway to where they had heard that Ulfcytel was with his levies. That was on Ascension Day, and at once the East Anglians fled. The men of Cambridgeshire stood firm against them. … The Danes had control of the field and there they were provided with horses, and afterwards had control of East Anglia, and ravaged and burnt that country for three months and even went into the wild fens, slaying the men and cattle, and burning throughout the fens; and they burnt down Thetford and Cambridge.

Again, the event was celebrated in Viking poetry, this time in praise of Olaf, by the poets Sighvat the Scald and Ottar the Black. The latter wrote:

I learn that your host, prince, far from the ships, piled up a heavy heap of slain. Ringmere Heath was reddened with blood. The people of the land, ere all was done, fell to the earth before you in the din of swords, and many a band of English fled terrified away.

The site of the battle, Ringmere, is (not for the first time) uncertain. It has been assumed to have been at Ringmere, a small lake near East Wretham, 6km north-east of Thetford, although more recently the suggestion has been made that it was Rymer in Suffolk.

By 1013 the pressure on Æthelred had grown so intense that Swein returned, intent not on yet another huge payoff but to take the kingdom of England itself. Swein's death that year, with one hand on the throne, led to his son Cnut succeeding him in charge of the Viking army. In 1016 Cnut won a decisive battle against the English at a place called *Assandun*, probably at Hadstock in Essex, in which among others, Ulfcytel was killed (Fig. 59). With the death of Æthelred's son and successor, Edmund Ironside, in the autumn, Cnut became undisputed king of all England and ruler of an Anglo-Danish empire. With it, England not only gained the relative peace its population craved, but a fresh wave of cultural influence from Scandinavia in general and Denmark in particular.

▼ Fig. 59
St Botolph's church Hadstock, Essex.

THE PEACE DIVIDEND

After all of the struggles of Æthelred's reign, and with the relative peace
following Cnut's accession to the throne, the eleventh century was one that
saw a centralising of control in kingship and the regulation of the whole of
England. This was seen most visibly in coinage, but also in the ever-increasing
wealth to be drawn from the land. With it emerged a burgeoning middle
or thegnly class, with an increasing interest in buying and selling land, and
patronising the Church (Fig. 60). In particular, we can see the development of
the parish system of churches that largely survives today.

Cnut was also active, becoming a patron of the Church and thereby helping
to ingratiate himself to one of the most powerful forces in Anglo-Saxon
society. It also helped him to present himself on the wider European stage
as a great and pious Christian ruler. East Anglia saw his involvement in the
establishment of two Benedictine monasteries, the most important of which
was at Bury St Edmunds (Fig. 61). The shrine that had first been established
at Bury to protect and venerate St Edmund's holy relics cannot have been any
later than the production of the Edmund memorial coinage from about the
mid-890s. However, the first documentary evidence possibly comes from a
land grant made by King Edmund of England, dated 945, while the will of
Bishop Theodred of London, made some time between 942-51, bequeathed
more land to the clerics there. However, the shrine remained in the hands of a
community of priests. Under Cnut, this was converted into a full monastery of
Benedictine monks.

The difference between the two types of community might seem rather
academic to a modern audience, but for the contemporary population
this change would have been seen as having wider political implications.
A major distinction was that the Benedictines lived according to a single,
fixed, monastic rule and took vows of celibacy and poverty. The widespread
adoption of Benedictine monastic life had been seen across Europe as a means
of tightening up on the perceived (or actual) laxity of some communities of
priests. It also tied the monks to the patronage of the crown more closely;
priestly communities tended to hold the lands of their church as 'prebends' or
personal holdings and, as they could marry, this often meant that land or rights
were passed on to a priest's son. Although there is uncertainty over Cnut's
role in the regularisation of Bury as a Benedictine monastery, he was certainly
responsible for the abbey church's reconsecration on October 18th 1032.
Making Bury an abbey therefore raised its status and allowed Cnut to patronise
a saint who was already of enormous importance: quite probably St Edmund
was the inspiration for the naming of Edmund Ironside, the king Cnut had

▲ Fig. 60

Large fragment from a cross shaft base in the Viking Mammen style, found when a house in Norwich, built on the site of the possible pre-Conquest church of St Vedast, was demolished in 1896. The cross demonstrates patronage of the Church by individuals using Scandinavian art styles.

defeated in battle in 1016. Bury's reconsecration therefore probably allowed Cnut to make a visible link between himself, a Danish king who had defeated an English king called Edmund in battle, just as a previous Viking leader, Ivar, had done in 869.

The other Benedictine monastery associated with, if not actually founded by, Cnut is St Benet at Holm in the parish of Horning, Norfolk (Fig. 62). Beloved by nineteenth-century landscape painters, this monastery is best known from its marshy location in the middle of Broadland. Its early origins are unclear. House traditions (like many other monasteries trying to create their own venerable history) record that an earlier community under an individual called Suneman was destroyed by the Vikings. Later, a hermit called Wulfric occupied the site and was recognised by Cnut who endowed a community here with the land of three manors. Cnut's role is likewise unclear although the landed endowment to St Benet's was quite possibly a royal estate. More intriguing is the tradition from a Bury St Edmunds document, the White Book (*Liber Albus*), that Bury's first monks were drawn from St Benet's under Cnut's direction.

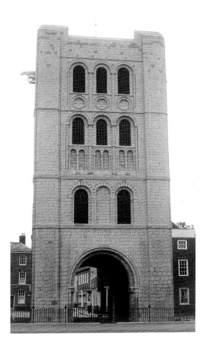

▲ Fig. 61

The Norman gatehouse to Bury St Edmunds abbey precinct, built under Abbot Anselm between 1120 and 1148.

▲ Fig. 62

The marshy island of Holm St Benets. The cross marks the position of the abbey church's high altar.

St Benet's certainly seems to have had various Danish connections. One of its early benefactors was Grimolf the Dane, who is recorded as being buried in the abbey church, and who had donated land and the church at Caister by Yarmouth to the abbey. To have been called 'the Dane' in an area with an Anglo-Scandinavian population suggests that Grimolf was one of Cnut's men, following his king in patronising the new monastery. Likewise, at the Norman Conquest in 1066, the abbot, Ælfwold, fled to Denmark. He was not alone. Another benefactor of St Benet's, Eadric the Steersman, gave land and the churches at Antingham, Calthorpe, Erpingham, Honing and Waxham; Domesday Book records that 'after King William came into England, this Eadric was an outlaw in Denmark'. However, a more intriguing link to Scandinavia is a small lead sheet found in a molehill at St Benet's in January 2003 (Fig. 63). Thanks to the finder being responsible and reporting his find, we can see that this apparent scrap has a story to tell.

Discovered near where the abbey church's high altar would have been, the sheet is inscribed with 49 runic letters, which seem to include Scandinavian rune-forms. Not only had runic inscriptions been all but abandoned by the English by the eleventh century, the inscription is meaningless, its letters forming gibberish. This is probably deliberate as other lead sheets with meaningless inscriptions are known from Scandinavia. Many are associated with churchyard burials, the gibberish probably being a form of 'charm language' like our magical word 'abracadabra'. The high altar would be exactly the place around which honoured members of St Benet's would be buried – people like Abbot Ælfwold or Grimolf. If use of a charm like this is a practice that was picked up in Scandinavia, it is not hard to see someone like Ælfwold bringing this tradition back with them. At the least, it provides another clear example of how the Viking world continued to influence not just designs of jewellery or metalwork, but the thoughts behind beliefs and practices.

◀ FIG. 63

FOLDED LEAD RUNIC SHEET FROM HOLM ST BENETS.

NEW ART FOR A NEW AGE

The metalwork of the eleventh century is as unequivocal as that of the tenth in showing the continued influence of Scandinavian art-styles on East Anglia and Anglo-Saxon England more widely. In particular this is associated with the use of two art styles, Ringerike and Urnes. Ringerike is the name of a district a few miles north of Oslo, from which various carved stones defined a new art style in the early eleventh century. It is particularly characterised by lively

FIG. 64 ▷
RINGERIKE STYLE BRIDLE CHEEKPIECE FRAGMENT
FROM GREAT WITCHINGHAM, NORFOLK.

animals with tendrils often sprouting from their heads and tails, often with a characteristic curl or 'flick' at the end. It can be seen on various pieces of metalwork, interestingly very often on horse-fittings, for instance bridle cheek-pieces such as an example from Great Witchingham (Fig. 64). This would once have formed part of a large double-headed plate, two heads projecting in the same direction top and bottom, joined at their necks. A large hole at this central point would have secured the bridle bit via a loop. A similar pair would then have been on the other side of the horse's mouth.

Other animal heads were similarly used to decorate stirrups, for instance cast copper-alloy terminals at the bottom angle of iron stirrup frames, like the wonderful example from Gooderstone with its typical Ringerike mane with curls (Fig. 65). The style was used on many other fittings, from brooches to buckles, such as the wonderful bird brooch from Stoke Holy Cross (Fig. 66). Equally significant, the style had wide-ranging appeal and was adopted on some high-status items, for example the large and expensive silver disc brooch found

▲ Fig. 65
COPPER-ALLOY STIRRUP TERMINAL FROM GOODERSTONE, NORFOLK.

▲ Fig. 66
BIRD BROOCH IN RINGERIKE STYLE FROM STOKE HOLY CROSS, NORFOLK.

◀ Fig. 67
THE SUTTON, ISLE OF ELY DISC BROOCH.
© *THE TRUSTEES OF THE BRITISH MUSEUM.*

in 1694 in Sutton on the Isle of Ely, as part of a gold and silver hoard (Fig. 67). Dating to the first half of the eleventh century, this appears to have been made for a woman as an inscription on the back records:

> Ædwen owns me, may the Lord own her. May the Lord curse him who takes me from her, unless she gives me of her own free will

Judged against other examples of Ringerike art – and perhaps surprising since it was such a large and ostentatious piece of silver jewellery – the brooch is quite crude. It is, though, interesting in combining this Viking style, such as the animals with their lobed snouts, with Anglo-Saxon elements like its overall design of interlocking circles with silver bosses. It shows very nicely the overlap or fusion of styles and the demand for this in even the upper reaches of society.

▲ Fig. 68
URNES STYLE STIRRUP-STRAP MOUNT FROM NORWICH.

Fig. 69 ▶

COPPER-ALLOY OPENWORK MOUNT IN URNES STYLE AND AN INTERPRETIVE DRAWING. *DRAWING BY SUE WHITE.*

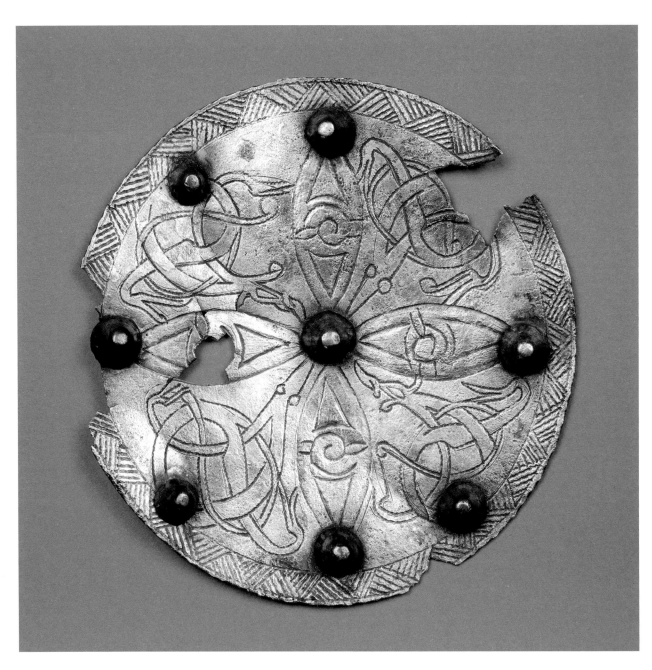

The last hurrah of Scandinavian art to be found in England came with the
Urnes style. Named after the vigorous carvings found on the wooden stave-
church of Urnes in Sogn province, Norway, it developed in the mid-eleventh
century and features sinuous animals intertwining with thin ribbons and often
each animal biting its neighbour. Urnes art was once again used on various
pieces of metalwork, for instance on stirrup-strap mounts (mounts placed over

the junction between the strap and loop of an iron stirrup), such as that from Norwich (Fig. 68). A curved mount from an uncertain object found in Elsing shows the complexity of the tendrils and limbs which can only be understood easily when shown in a line drawing (Fig. 69 a and b).

The popularity of the Urnes style can be seen by its use on not only everyday items but high-status commissions, for instance another silver disc-brooch, found in Bredfield, Suffolk (Fig. 70). Found by a metal-detectorist in 2009 and measuring about 105mm in diameter, the brooch is made from a silver sheet and incised with decoration. It shows a development from the Sutton brooch as, although still decorated with silver bosses and the pointed oval fields stretching out as a cross from the central boss, the spaces in between are occupied by two pairs of opposing creatures. One pair has oval eyes, open mouths and tendrils, as viewed from the side; the other pair has long snouts and circular eyes to either side, as though being viewed from above. The animals clearly derive from an English version of the Urnes style. As interesting is the outer border which has a cross-hatched or plait motif, that is also seen in twelfth-century architecture, for instance over the door to the round-towered Essex church of Great Leighs (Fig. 71). This itself has parallels in the tower of Neukirchen (Kreis Eutin), Schleswig-Holstein, an area formerly within the Viking Age kingdom of Denmark.

Fig. 71 ▷

TOWER WEST DOOR OF GREAT LEIGHS, ESSEX, WITH THE PLAIT MOTIF ON ITS HOOD-MOULD.

◄ Fig. 72

Norwich cathedral cloister capital using Urnes style decoration. © *Roland Harris.*

The Bredfield brooch is therefore a wonderful example of how a rich East Anglian chose to dress at the end of the Anglo-Saxon period, drawing upon the prevailing artistic styles being used in Scandinavia. A preference for such Anglo-Scandinavian culture was clearly part of received local tradition, reinforced by a second wave of influence unleashed by Cnut's conquest, especially in the Danelaw. This influence was stubbornly to remain. While the political involvement of Scandinavia was to wane in the years after the Norman Conquest of 1066, the Vikings' cultural legacy took longer to disappear. Even as late as the twelfth century, when Norwich Cathedral was being constructed by the Normans in their Romanesque style and from stone imported from Caen in Normandy, there was room for expressions of this residual culture. The Urnes style is prominent in at least one of the capitals used in the cathedral cloister (Fig. 72). The fineness of the carving not only attests to the skill of the sculptor but their familiarity with the style, suggesting its maintained popularity in at least this part of East Anglia. Norwich Cathedral was a flagship construction project for the incoming Norman elite: large, bold, and part of their vision for a new England. And yet, it could not help but include traces of the northern ancestry of the population it was built to serve and dominate.

EPILOGUE: WHAT DID THE VIKINGS EVER DO FOR US?

From their first speculative raids on the East coast, to full-blooded military campaigning and subsequent settlement, the Vikings made a highly visible impact upon Anglo-Saxon England. While the so-called Second Viking Age with renewed raids and conquest under Cnut may be seen as more overtly political, its occurrence followed a well-trodden path leading to a new influx of Scandinavians settling and ruling in England. As ever, East Anglia was at the heart of these events and with its geographical position, long coastline and wealthy landscape was both convenient and attractive.

Throughout, the Vikings held a particular spell over contemporaries through the terror they inspired, revulsion at their heathen nature and the destruction and looting of Christian sites - yet also begrudging respect or awe for their military capacities. Much like modern audiences continue to be captivated by crime stories, or tales of notorious murderers, the mafia and pirates, so too the Vikings have preserved a sense of awe and fascination. They have become a byname for toughness or the warrior spirit, and perfect for taking as the name for a spirited enterprise or perhaps the nickname to a local rugby club as with North Walsham 'Vikings' (Fig. 73). They inspire people to re-enact their lives dressing in replicas of their clothes, using similar tools and jewellery. This can lead to genuine insights into the ways everyday objects may have been used, beyond the theoretical suggestions made by desk-bound museum curators or university lecturers. It can also be a lot of fun, providing the public with festivals featuring characterisations, or perhaps feeding our preconceptions, of what we want the Vikings to be (Fig. 74).

▲ FIG. 73

A MODERN-DAY 'VIKING'?
© HYWEL JONES AND NORTH WALSHAM RUGBY CLUB.

▲ FIG. 74

A BOAT-BURNING ON THE BEACH MARKS THE CULMINATION OF SHERINGHAM'S VIKING FESTIVAL.

Perhaps most important, clearly the Vikings still matter to us: they still have the power to speak to us and to allow us to create new meanings and our own truths for who or what they were. East Anglia may not bask in the better-known fame of York or Dublin for its Viking heritage, but as archaeology is showing, it has an ancestry just as strong. However East Anglians choose to define themselves today or in the future, that Viking background is undeniably one of the region's major building blocks, ever present in the names of our villages or the landscape they settled in and helped to create (Fig. 75). It provides a fitting legacy to an area that continues to provide a home to many newly incoming people, settling among an existing East Anglia population today, just as it did over a thousand years ago.